THE LOGIC THAT GOD EXISTS

THE LOGIC THAT GOD EXISTS

A HANDBOOK ON BELIEF IN GOD
THROUGH SIMPLE REASON
TO BRING YOU PEACE

ROBERT B. TRUSSELL

SOPHIA INSTITUTE PRESS
Manchester, New Hampshire

Copyright © 2024 by Robert B. Trussell

Printed in the United States of America. All rights reserved.

Edited by Anne Trussell Nunley

Cover and interior design by KUHN Design Group

No part of this book may be reproduced, stored in a retrieval system, or transmitted in any form, or by any means, electronic, mechanical, photocopying, or otherwise, without the prior written permission of the publisher, except by a reviewer, who may quote brief passages in a review.

Sophia Institute Press
Box 5284, Manchester, NH 03108
1-800-888-9344
www.SophiaInstitute.com

Sophia Institute Press is a registered trademark of Sophia Institute.

paperback ISBN 979-8-88911-348-5

ebook ISBN 979-8-88911-349-2

Library of Congress Control Number: 2024936977

First printing

This book is dedicated to the wonderful family of my parents, the great gift of my wife and children and a special thanks to Martha, Anne, and Lisa for their help. It is also dedicated to all my atheist friends and all nonbelievers, that they may believe.

CONTENTS

Preface vii

PART 1
How I Know There is a God

1. "Everything Just Happened by Itself" 5
2. My Story 7
3. Evolution: the God Replacement? 11
4. Scientism — the Given 15
5. Existence of God 19
6. Laws of Nature 23
7. Pascal's Wager 29
8. Jesus: "Who Do You Say That I Am?" 33
9. Review: Existence of God 43

PART 2
From Reason to Faith

10. Going Deeper: Faith 49
11. What If You Were God? 55
12. Barriers to Belief 63
13. Miracles, Miracles, and My Tempur-Pedic Miracle 71
14. God Makes Deals with His People 77
15. Why Are We Here? (Hint: It's a Test) 79

PART 3
Creation and Christianity

16. The Christian View of Creation	85
17. The Bible: God Talks to Us	107
18. Prayer: We Talk to God	115
19. Free Will	119
20. The Secret to Life	123
21. Summary: Our Stairway to Heaven	127
Afterword	133
About the Author	137

PREFACE

This little book is for anyone without strong faith, or any faith at all, in the existence of God. It's for atheists, agnostics, and those who believe in God—or at least the idea of God—but are weak in their faith. In other words, it's for just about everybody. Think of it as a handbook for why we should believe in God and what that means for our lives.

A recent Gallup Poll revealed that the number of Americans who believe in God has fallen to 81% from 98% in the 1960s. When asked if they were "convinced" God exists, the 81% number is more like 60% today. In Europe and Scandinavia this number is about 15%.

Similarly, survey after survey has shown that the "nones"—the religiously unaffiliated—are increasing dramatically in our culture. It has become the default position of young people, our educators, and the media. Forty percent of those under the age of 40 have no religious affiliation. Many people simply never think about these things.

I should pause to clarify here—when I reference "God" I'm speaking of a personal, Judeo-Christian God, as commonly understood from the Bible. Not a nebulous "higher power," new age "energy," or watered-down abstract deity. I aim to defend the biblical God, because

I believe diminishing interpretations dishonor His true nature and identity.

In my view, the existence of God is the most important question for humanity to contemplate. Since the dawn of time and for millennia, man has fundamentally believed in some interpretation of God. But modern uncertainty has muddied the waters. More people now than ever live and die without resolving this essential question, contributing to a global crisis in identity and societal turmoil. In our sophisticated age, basic truths are being obscured and forgotten, causing many to question whether we need God at all. And yet, given the chaos of the modern day, does mankind truly appear in control of this world?

Whether or not you believe in God profoundly shapes your opinions and worldview. Given the same facts and scenarios, people will draw radically different conclusions based on their perspective of ultimate truth. This explains totally contradictory views on what should be straightforward modern issues that exist in our political sphere. A biblical worldview simplifies such matters; removing God complicates even basic truths.

Given the title of this book, you may have guessed the answer to the question, "Does God exist?" The answer would be YES!—according to me, anyway. But I come at this from a slightly different perspective than you may be thinking. I believe God has equipped us to understand this from a rational perspective, not just a faith perspective. This may appeal to some and not to others, but I believe it's immensely helpful to look at this question logically and even scientifically.

The point of this book is to show that there is ample and compelling evidence that there is a God, and further that Jesus was God and is God. Contrary to some who say there's no evidence, I maintain the opposite—**it is impossible that there is not a God.**

The best news is that this completely changes your outlook on life if you understand and embrace the fact that Jesus is Lord to you. He created you and is with you throughout your life and will be with you through eternity. In this context, all the problems in your life are seen in a new light—the light of truth, trust, and salvation.

The purpose of this book is not to win an argument against nonbelievers. If that's all it is, I haven't accomplished much. It is to bring order to your life as you align yourself with the Ultimate Order within a community of believers, a team dedicated to truth, beauty, and service, giving you a sense of belonging.

As you've often heard television preachers say, it's to "accept Jesus Christ as your personal Lord and Savior." They are right! But I can see where that might be a bridge too far for many at first. The important thing is your direction. Baby steps. And for many, the first baby step is acknowledging the overwhelming evidence for the existence of God.

THE LOGIC THAT GOD EXISTS

PART 1

HOW I KNOW THERE IS A GOD

CHAPTER 1

"EVERYTHING JUST HAPPENED BY ITSELF"

There is a widespread concept embedded within our culture that "everything just happened by itself" about how the 8 billion people running around the surface of this globe came to be. This concept gradually took hold about 150 years ago mainly because of Darwin's Theory of Evolution, which then greatly influenced the Age of Enlightenment, the precursor of current Western civilization. It says that the building blocks of life started very small and then advanced through natural selection and, over millions of years, became what we now see. The ramifications of this idea are the root of many of the problems we face today. It is entrenched in the culture, manifestly false, and should be removed from cultural orthodoxy.

BLOWING UP GRAVEYARDS

Let's exclude faith for now and employ reason alone, so no faith required, much less blind faith!

I once told an atheist friend about a mathematician I'd read about who calculated the odds of life randomly forming as equivalent to blowing up a graveyard and the explosions reconfiguring into a working space shuttle. He glibly replied, "Well, if you blow up enough graveyards…"

That exchange captures the crux of disagreement between atheism and faith. No quantity of explosions could transform cemetery remnants into an operational spacecraft. It's impossible and any reasonable mind should be able to admit such improbability. The atheist must contend it be so, however.

Nonbelievers, ask yourselves: What is the source of your disbelief? Do you want to believe, but you feel unable? Or do you resist belief?

Either way, many readily trust science over Scripture, or never contemplate these concerns. Some of us just seem to have a strong faith in the existence of God naturally. Some of us are just the opposite. Many of us will say we believe, but faith is weak and often forgotten in our daily lives. Meanwhile, the culture constantly whispers, "Don't believe, don't believe!" We don't have enough conviction to say, "Wait a minute, that doesn't reconcile with what I believe."

It's interesting to think that according to Christian teaching, we are judged much more by what we believe than what we do. Christ's message was, "I'll forgive you if you forgive others." But the consequences are not so good if you don't believe. So, if you can get past this one thing—everything just happened by itself—you're well on your road to a different outlook on life, peace, and ultimately salvation. I will show you. It's pretty easy because it couldn't have been any other way.

> **Important:** Refrain from letting the culture make up your mind for you.

CHAPTER 2

MY STORY

I was a senior in college, and despite a thorough Christian upbringing, I had not been going to church except when I went home, and my mother made me go. I was driving along one day musing about such things, and I asked myself, "Well, Bob, after all the education and spiritual direction from Mom, do you believe there is a God or not? And do you believe in the basic tenets of the Catholic Church or not?" I thought for a few minutes and then said, "Well, I guess I really do."

It was not a moment of inspiration or deep religious experience. It was merely an honest moment where I questioned myself. But it was also in that moment that whether I liked it or not, this had changed how I would live my life going forward.

Yes, I am a believer, and that meant being bound by specific rules beginning with the Ten Commandments. This was not instant, and I did not even start going to church right away (or for many years, actually), but nevertheless, a seed was planted that day.

When I was thinking about how I would answer my own question, I knew that if I said, "No, I don't believe it," I would immediately get hit with another question from myself, which was, *why not?*

That point was going to be challenging to answer. And it's a question people should ask themselves and others. If you don't believe in God, **why the heck not?**

If you don't, then you are a card-carrying member of the "Everything just happened by itself club," and you've just taken a position that's far more difficult to defend to yourself or others than the fact that there is a Creator who built everything we see. And when I say everything, I mean everything.

Because if there's one thing in all the trillions of functions that promote life, just one thing that did not happen by itself, then everything did *not* happen by itself—and there is a God.

So, dear reader, if *something* did not happen by itself, that means *somebody* had started everything, or at least kicked the ball rolling. A Creator, which is the same thing as saying God.

So, you're already there. The First Mover. There *must* be one unless ... everything just happened by itself.

Now, that wasn't so hard actually.

If you accept this pretty simple logic, at the minimum, you are now a Deist, and you have joined the ranks of Thomas Jefferson, Benjamin Franklin, and Neil Armstrong. They believed that there had to be a God because of human reason, but they did not believe He revealed Himself or that He is involved in the world. They knew from reason that everything could not happen by itself, and that's where it ended for them. I call it a minimalist belief in God but nevertheless a belief in a Divine Creator.

It's the same way with Jesus. If you don't believe Jesus is who He said He was, what exactly is it that you don't believe? Where do you get off the Jesus train?

So maybe by now you're starting to see how there really *has* to be a God, a Creator of everything, and that everything didn't happen by itself. But if that's true, why does there seem to be such a randomness in life, and why do all these bad things happen? Why are we not protected by this God if He is a benevolent one?

CHAPTER 3

EVOLUTION: THE GOD REPLACEMENT?

We are conditioned to believe that "science" is the only field that is important, or even real. Studies like philosophy and theology have been tossed out the window amid cultural cries of "follow the science" when in fact, if there is a God, He created science in the first place.

Truthfully, science alone has no answer to how plants, animals, and humans came to be. It also has no explanation as to *why*.

Why would a bunch of atoms bumping into each other end up creating a squirrel? Why would there even be a bunch of atoms? Why would randomness beget order? Why would randomness beget rules?

The idea of survival of the fittest implies that survival is good. In the random universe, why would survival be good? There would be no purpose. And the more you think about it — how could anyone believe that this is what's happened?

We've been conditioned to believe that everything just happened by itself, but it did not. **There is no way.** Evolution has been ingrained in our minds, but it was never meant to explain how the universe got to where it is. It was meant to explain animals and how they changed over time. It was extended to include everything! Atheistic scientists speak of natural selection by chemicals. Huh?

Again, why would there even be a survival instinct without a guiding hand? Who wants to survive?

Look at the human body and its incredible complexity. Think about what it takes just to move your finger. You must do it through thought, which generates electrical impulses through a maze of nerves from your head to your hand and then stimulates more nerves and a pulley system of muscle, bone, and tendons to move that finger precisely to the intended length.

This is just one of thousands of body functions that go on intentionally or behind the scenes to regulate our body every second of the day.

How could this happen by itself? There are literally not enough graveyards to blow up, or eons since the beginning of time to try.

The theory of evolution has conditioned us to believe that everything just happened by itself, with some inborn process. But this cannot be true. Just because birds, for instance, evolve into different species does not mean that a rock could develop into a human. The evolution of a bird into a slightly different bird is called microevolution. Evidence of macroevolution from a bird to another species over time is very scarce.

While there is no doubt that there are many examples of microevolution where species evolve based upon favorable genetic mutations that lend advantage and, therefore, survival, it is tough to come up with examples of macroevolution where major species evolved into a different significant species.

Importantly, no evidence or theory exists of how this could work from inanimate objects growing into animate ones. People started thinking, if a saber-toothed tiger can evolve into a modern-day cat, then we all could have just come from the Big Bang somehow or an electric storm charging some matter, which turned it into a human being over time, à la Frankenstein. No!

No intermediate fossil forms have been found for macroevolution from one species to another. The fossil record shows no evidence of simple life forms transitioning into complex life forms. Instead, there was a virtual explosion of animal types during the Cambrian era. Most of those have stayed the same to this day.

Natural selection does exist for relatively small variations within species. But how could it account for the eye, for example, with all the minimal incremental steps? The benefit of the measures would only be advantageous once the eye was fully formed millions of years later.

Darwinian evolution has caused scientists to explain things strictly physically and view human behavior as an extension in degree—not in kind—of lower animal behavior. They have no concept of soul.

The immensely influential Italian philosopher and priest, St. Thomas Aquinas, said that the soul is: 1) immaterial; 2) subsists by itself; and 3) is not dependent on matter for existence.

To understand the essence of all corporeal (bodily) things, the intellect must be outside of corporeal things. It cannot already be any corporeal thing. No material organ, not even the human brain, can self-reflect. Such proper and complete self-reflection must be the truly spiritual act of a truly spiritual soul.

But can the evolutionary process naturally produce a spiritual soul? No!

St. Thomas goes on to say that since the human soul is not dependent on corporeal matter, its origin transcends what is sufficient to produce organic forms. The only causality adequate to make the spiritual soul is "creation." And to create something out of nothing, the "agent" must be infinite, i.e., God. This direct causality is the only adequate explanation for the human soul's origin.

God animates us through our soul the way electricity animates a light bulb or waves animate a radio. It is invisible, but we know it's there by its actions. If you see a coat hanging on the back of the door, you can't see the hook, but you know it's there. Similarly, we know God exists because of His creation. We know He exists because of how we are protected and that this could never have happened all by itself. Scientists have discovered the laws of nature, **but someone had to make the laws**. Laws don't make themselves.

Our culture has replaced God with something else. Evolution has become our God.

CHAPTER 4

SCIENTISM – THE GIVEN

When you read the news, the headlines are usually written from the perspective that "Everything just happened by itself," and we evolved from nothing. "Scientists discover…" meaning they want you to think that science is everything and that philosophy and religion are irrelevant.

This is called scientism. It's the default in our media and culture. Science seems to make things like the biblical Adam and Eve story look ridiculous. But we know that all three are valid. The challenge is reconciling them, not throwing religion and philosophy out the window.

University of Miami Philosophy Professor Susan Haack goes a step further, saying that scientism is "an exaggerated kind of deference toward science, an excessive readiness to accept as authoritative any claim made by the sciences, and to dismiss every kind of criticism of science or its practitioners as anti-scientific prejudice."

Such scientific extremism could be described as a sort of religious radicalism. Indeed, scientism is often used to explain away the existence of God. Also, what can science tell you about ethics, beauty, what is good, what is true? That answer would be zero.

Dennis Bonnette's brilliant *Origin of the Human Species* states, "evolution theory is a philosophy of atheistic naturalism, not science. Since there is no God, there is no possible supernatural intervention, and experiential data demands an evolutionary rationale. Therefore, life must arise from non-life by some natural process. The question is not 'if' but 'how.' And since it happened once, it must have happened many times, given the vastness and age of the universe."

We've made wonderful scientific discoveries, especially over the past century, which means science is always changing. Right? But you hear: "the science is settled."

Famous clinical psychologist and author Jordan Peterson states, "Belief in science is dogma on something that's constantly changing. The religious enterprise doesn't only emphasize rationality, it brings in music, arts, drama, literature, architecture, and the entire essence of what it means to be human. It includes the organizing of cities around a central point. It manifests itself across multiple dimensions of human existence simultaneously, bringing a richness that cannot be diluted without loss."

Religion provides the sacred, holding society together. Conversely, atheism is rather boring.

Have you ever noticed the headlines always seem to say, "scientists were surprised" to discover this or that? Well, religion and philosophy don't change so much. They're products of what G.K. Chesterton called the *democracy of the dead*: thousands of years of living and tradition. There's a great danger in thinking that our ancestors were dumb and we are smart. Technology makes us feel superior when, in many ways, the opposite is true, and we have lost much of the wisdom of our forefathers while our culture is deteriorating. Those people of old were often far more grounded and closer to God than our culture is today. We must be careful not to be so smart that we're dumb. Self-help authors can often be this way.

Does it make sense to say that science, which is still poorly understood, is the only thing that is legitimate, and therefore, religion and philosophy are of no account? This thought process replaces an unchanging God with something ever-changing. If there is a God—which this book will conclusively show—why would we do this?

In essence, there are only two worldviews that people have. Either there is an all-powerful God who created the universe and created us, or "everything just kind of happened by itself."

Which one are you? You must choose one. And if you choose the "everything happened by itself" view, you must be honest about *why* in view of the scientific and mathematical data showing how impossible this is.

For instance, how do we reconcile the Adam and Eve story with modern-day science, which uses mitochondria DNA evidence to show that man has been around for hundreds of thousands of years and that we descended from primates? This is a fascinating question, and it is the correct question. We should not say let's embrace one that we don't fully understand and disparage the other. Again, the correct question is how do we reconcile them?

> *The special creation of true humans would be manifest by the first clear signs of true human behavior, not by some fossil phenomenon. Catholic teaching insists on monogenism vs polygenism, meaning evolution through a single pair of*

> *individuals vs many. A bottleneck. Most evolutionists would say this is possible but unlikely, given their lack of philosophical perspective. The infusion of a soul into an advanced primate's body would radically transform and animate it.*
>
> *A second alternative would be a similar effect in the embryonic stage. The non-human primate parents could quickly raise the human children.*
>
> *Theistic evolution proponents should incorporate the clear scriptural point of direct divine intervention and not just say God oversaw this gradual evolution.*
>
> *Further, the Genesis story could be literally true, leaving the scientific record to confuse and humble the intellectually proud.*
>
> **DENNIS BONNETTE**, *Origin of the Human Species*

The point here is not to solve this question on these pages but to point out that there are ways to reconcile the biblical account of creation with the science we know today. **We know that both are true.**

Looking at the physical world as we know it, the two main concepts that Man has come up with to explain how we all got here are both impossible! I'm speaking of science and philosophy. Neither science nor philosophy can explain how we sprang from nothing, with no guiding hand, to what we see today.

Yet here we are. Only religion can explain it. But to believe in religion, you must start by believing in God.

CHAPTER 5

EXISTENCE OF GOD

It's fashionable to say that you cannot prove the existence of God. However, it is also true that we cannot prove that He does *not* exist.

To atheists, it may seem likely or possible that God does not exist, but nevertheless, no one can prove it. Therefore, God may exist, right? The question becomes, does the order we see in the universe come from order, which means intelligence, or did it come from randomness? Were we able to blow up enough graveyards so the pieces dissolved into the space shuttle? It comes down to probabilities.

If you could prove that truly random particles in space bouncing around with energy could easily create a protein or amino acid, programmed to survive, then it would be easy to conclude that we could have come from randomness. But if you can't prove that you swing the other way rather quickly and realize that an intelligent entity had to create the order we see.

Again, this comes darn close to proving the existence of God. If you can disprove the randomness theory of our existence, that pretty much proves the existence of God because it's the only other alternative.

The graveyard analogy is patently impossible. Now, one might say that a space shuttle is manufactured with plastics and all sorts of man-made parts. Okay. How about the graveyard dust coming down to form ... a working elephant? Most people would say no, it's never gonna happen, no matter how many years go by.

The beauty of this is it all comes down to mathematics. In *The Unreasonable Effectiveness of Mathematics in the Natural Sciences*, Eugene Wigner writes, "The miracle of the appropriateness of the language of mathematics for the formulation of the laws of physics is a wonderful gift which we neither understand nor deserve."

Mathematicians such as Wigner will tell you that there has not been enough time elapsed for random particles to, by accident, form one amino acid, the building blocks for proteins, which are the building blocks for life. Furthermore, even if it did beat the odds and included an amino acid, there are no instructions for that amino acid to design it to develop into anything else or even to keep existing. You would need another graveyard event to take this tiniest second step. It can't happen by itself. If there's no God, there's no inborn momentum for survival, much less improvement, whether we're talking about atoms bouncing around or the building blocks of life.

We are being force-fed a singular evolutionary theory by scientists, the media, governments, and academia. The fact is it is just a theory, and there are competing theories we rarely hear about. Conventional wisdom is often wrong.

Laws of Probability cast tremendous doubt on the possibility that base amino acids necessary for life evolved.

If you have a dinner party for 20 people and you're making name tags for where people should sit, how many different possible seating arrangements are there?

The answer is: 2 million trillion different seating arrangements. (It's 20 factorial, 20 x 19 x 18, you can Google it.)

Consider next that there is "dissymmetry" in a protein molecule, meaning the atoms are not evenly scattered as one would expect if it happened without guidance. *They are arranged!*

So, the next question is, how many atoms are there in a protein molecule?

Answer? At least 100, up to thousands. So now I have a "dinner party" with at least 100 people. How many different seating arrangements are there now?

Answer? *9 trillion trillion trillion trillion trillion trillion trillion.*

Since the beginning, there are not enough atoms in the universe or time for this to happen only by chance.

Former President Ronald Reagan remarked once that he has been unable to understand the atheist in this world of so much beauty and he had an unholy desire to invite some atheists to a dinner with the most fabulous gourmet dinner ever concocted and invite them and after the dinner ask them: *Do you think there was a cook?*

What about the primordial soup from which we all sprung? No cook?

Similarly, Dr. James Kennedy of Coral Ridge Ministries told a story about a person who set up in his basement the most amazing model of our solar system with the various moons going around the planets and the planets circulating the Sun. An atheist friend came over and was astounded by the model's complexity and accuracy. He said, "Who made this wonderful thing?" The man replied, "Nobody. I just walked down into my basement, and there it was!"

No, a gourmet meal must have a cook, a painting must have a

painter, a building must have a builder, and a watch must have a watchmaker. These things are obvious even to a child.

But who is the cook and where did he come from? Some may ask who created the Creator? The answer is the Prime Mover always was and always will be. He is existence itself and describes Himself as **I Am Who Am**. It's hard for us to understand this but God exists outside of time and is the One who created time as we know it. I picture this as God looking at a tiny globe which is the physical world that He created. He is external to this but part of it at the same time. As we were taught in school the answer to the question of "Where is God?" is "God is everywhere." Correct!

CHAPTER 6

LAWS OF NATURE

The problem with atheism is, according to science, there is no way it can be true. Matter can't create itself in the first place, and even if it could, it would just be a formless disorder with no rules and no laws of nature. Forget about developing into human life. There's no programming because there would be no programmer.

Science is all about logic. Logic dictates that something cannot come from nothing. **Therefore, science itself dictates that there has to be a God.**

Now, you might say that despite all the reasoning that everything couldn't have happened by itself, you think somehow it did anyway. And some scientists will always tell you that it could happen. But they can't tell you that the laws of nature made themselves. A First Cause had to make those laws; otherwise, the universe would have only mayhem. For instance, gravity accelerates at 32 feet per second per second. By understanding this law and other laws of aerodynamics and physics, we can make airplanes fly. These laws are constants everywhere in the universe. Some may try to say that the rules always were in force and, therefore, they are the god. But to say that is the desperation of logic.

The fact that the complexity, symmetry, and function of the laws of nature could not have happened by itself is self-evident. It is not rocket science, but the rocket-scientist type of people have the hardest time understanding it. Most people in man's history have innately understood this, but now it's almost become controversial to think that the world as we see it was created by God and not by mere happenstance. Some view us as extremists!

It should be easy to understand that the laws of nature that run the universe could not have made themselves. That's because it is easy to see that everything had to be completely random before the laws. Chaos! In society, we see that readily. If there are no laws or they are not adhered to, everything becomes random and chaotic.

The laws of gravity, speed of light, and boiling point of water are critical to our existence. These laws didn't just happen. God created them; as we will see, He had us in mind when He made them.

ATHEISM

The laws of nature argument is enough to convince many that there must be a God. Are you convinced?

Maybe you are an atheist and don't know it. Some people say they believe in God if asked, but their faith is so weak that they act the same as the nonbelievers. Believing in God should lead to *changing your worldview.*

Ludwig Feuerbach (nineteenth century) said that we invented God as a crutch, and, unfortunately, greatly influenced Karl Marx and Friedrich Nietzsche. He said if there were no God, we would invent him anyway. Answer: we would not have invented the God we understand to exist, perfect and threatening our lifestyle and eventual afterlife with judgment.

Often, when you confront atheists with the fact that it's impossible for the universe to be so ordered and for life to evolve the way it has because there simply hasn't been enough time for it to randomly happen, they are forced to come up with arcane counter theories. Somebody hatched the idea of the multiverse where they say okay, there wasn't enough time for this to happen randomly in our universe, but what if there were trillions and trillions and trillions of universes? Then all you need is one of then to randomly become us. But this theory has been widely discredited. Or they say well we descended from aliens, so we didn't have to evolve randomly like we have on Earth. But they need to follow through with the logic of how the aliens somehow evolved from nothing with no guiding hand.

When atheism first gained some popularity in the Victorian Age (1850-1900), its personal dimension was troubling. How could an atheist's oath of allegiance be trusted? It couldn't, so an atheist was not allowed to take a seat in Parliament. If you are unconstrained by fear of eternal punishment, you could not be held accountable to social norms of behavior. Atheism was not respectable.

> *When people stop believing in God, the problem is not that they will believe in nothing; rather, the problem is that they will believe anything.*
>
> **ATTRIBUTED TO G. K. CHESTERTON**

Nature abhors a vacuum. And when it comes to a belief system, humanity will always seek to fill a void in their hearts with a quest to live out their lives predicated upon a belief in something higher than themselves. Everyone yearns to believe in something, but if their belief system is untethered to their Creator, it leads to all sorts of problems and misery.

DNA

Our generation is very familiar with computers, composed of hardware and software. When famous Russian chess champion Gary Kasparov challenged the big blue IBM computer in 1996, he pitted his own intelligence against the software developers at IBM. Similarly, today, when we open up Windows on a laptop or our iPhone, we access the work of thousands of programmers at Microsoft or Apple.

Our DNA is the software that runs our bodies, our hardware. While it takes thousands of programmers to write software for Microsoft or Apple, are we to believe that our own infinitely more complex DNA software was supposed to have been written by no one? It just happened by itself?

NO, THERE HAD TO BE A PROGRAMMER

Evolution is a theory in crisis, and DNA accounts for part of that crisis. DNA is highly specified, functional genetic information. It has a four-character digital code, just like in a computer program. DNA contains complex specified instructions for how to build life. Who wrote the code?

Even the first living mono cell required complex code, as did every other kind of life that came along. New animals? You need new code and fast forward all the way down to the human brain. The human brain is the most complex thing we've discovered in the universe, and human DNA contains a vast, complex, functional, four-character digital code specifying exactly how the brain develops and works.

AGAIN, WHO WROTE THE CODE?

It takes about 2 billion lines of unique handwritten code by more than 25,000 engineers and a vast empire of computers and data centers spread throughout the entire globe to run Google.

But it takes more than 3 billion letters of unique genetic code arranged in a precise, specific manner, written inside a cell weighing 2,000 millionths of a gram, to run YOU, a far more complex and superior system than all of Google. Imagine looking at all that Google code and then me telling you it all evolved together on its own somehow. So, what makes more sense? That life and intelligence and the ability to think and love come from something that has life and intelligence and thinks and loves or that it comes from … random chaos.

THIS IS PROOF OF GOD! GAME OVER!

When you start to look at the world with a different eye—which sees that the world did not just happen by itself but is the product of a Creator—you realize that while you lose the idea of a dry, hopeless, universal spontaneous evolution, you gain an appreciation for the wonder and majesty of God. It may be amazing to think that all this just happened by itself, but to think that somebody had the intelligence and the vastness to have created it from thin air is much more amazing.

But now we must contemplate what it means for our life if we really believe in God. People don't want to contemplate this, and that is often the basis for their unbelief. Things like the Ten Commandments come quickly into play. It makes us consider our ultimate future and be a little more serious about life.

CHAPTER 7

PASCAL'S WAGER

What if it's all true?

Blaise Pascal was a famous French mathematician, physicist, inventor, writer, and Catholic philosopher. He is widely known for his argument known as Paschal's Wager: if it's a given that no one knows what happens when we die, any wise gambler would bet that Christianity is true and live life accordingly. If he's wrong, he ends up in the same place as the skeptic, if right he has Heaven as the winnings.

Have you ever been wrong about anything? This is the one we have to get right, and it should be easy to err on the side of caution!

We distract ourselves from these great questions. It's like we're playing gin rummy on a train, hurtling down the tracks with the upcoming bridge out. Should we focus on the gin rummy game or the fact that the bridge is out?

And then how many of us deny God's existence but then curse Him anyway? How do you stand with God?

We are called to repent and to reform. Change your way of thinking. Your way of thinking is probably wrong! The reign of God is at hand. The Kingdom is at hand.

Pascal's Wager does not prove the existence of God, but it shows the logic of believing in God even if it's difficult. It recognizes that we start from the position that even though we don't know if there is a God, it is a no-brainer to believe anyway because the consequences of not believing are high risk. And this is not a lie where you really don't believe and just say you do. It's admitting that you don't know but recognize the possibility of the existence of the Christian God, and you say yes to the *possibility*.

Again, what if it's all true? You don't want to die, and the first thing you do is meet Jesus and think: *Oh, no.*

I know people who are very risk-averse in this world but are atheists or agnostics. So, they're afraid to take risks in this world, but they'll roll the dice on eternity because they are sure they know the outcome (which is counter to what humankind has always believed); this is called pride.

This high stakes gamble is unnecessary, and to me, is a fast train to Stupidsville.

Let's say you still don't believe in God and have rejected His efforts to reach out to you during your life and to get you to seek Him. At the moment of death, guess what's going to happen? At this point, you'll hope you were right and **will be rooting for there to be nothing!**

But what if you lose the bet and are standing there before Jesus? You're going to choose hell! Why would you change?

Now, we don't know God's mind, which is so much above our minds, and maybe we get a chance to say, "Jesus, if I had only believed in You, I would have picked You," and God may still relent and show His infinite mercy. But per Pascal, why not do that down here? If it might be true, what do we have to lose? Take that insurance policy.

Someone might even say that it is a sin to play fast and loose with your soul, which, like everything else, is a gift from God. If you don't accept Pascal's Wager, that's what you are doing — playing fast and loose with your most valuable possession and eternal state.

There are more steps because now we have to figure out who is God? Besides being the Creator of everything, which is hard even to contemplate, who is He?

CHAPTER 8

JESUS: "WHO DO YOU SAY THAT I AM?"

So now I'm going to assume that all the arguments I just made fell on deaf ears. You're saying no, Bob, everything *did* happen by itself, and it makes sense that our DNA coded itself somehow. Okay. Let's prove the existence of God in a completely different way.

We've barely mentioned Jesus, who is the manifestation of God in the physical world, flesh and blood. Jesus said unequivocally that he was the Son of God and the Son of Man and that he was indeed God—and He backed it up in spades.

This distinguishes Christianity from all other major religions today, including Buddhism, Hinduism, Islam, and Judaism. Jesus claims divinity and is the only one of these major religions to do so.

There are those of you who think that the Bible stories are just stories, and that Jesus might not have even existed. But you must consider that Jesus is the most monumental figure in history. This makes it very unlikely that He wasn't real. His followers followed Him to the ends of the Earth and proclaimed His name everywhere. We measure time around the birth of Christ. The Bible itself describes in great detail the birth, life, death, and resurrection of Jesus. It is the most copied, read, and distributed book in the history of mankind. The Old Testament is the basis for Christianity, Judaism, and Islam. And we have many non-biblical sources supporting the existence of Jesus.

The first non-Christian author to mention Jesus is thought to be the Jewish historian Flavius Josephus (born Yosef ben Matityahu), who wrote a history of Judaism in about the year 93, the famous *Antiquities of the Jews*. In his writings, he mentions several figures from the New Testament, including Jesus, John the Baptist, and Jesus's "brother" James.

The following passage, in which Josephus mentions Jesus and his "brother" James, firmly establishes the existence of Jesus outside of the Bible:

> *Festus was now dead, and Albinus was but upon the road; so he [Ananus] assembled the Sanhedrin of judges, and brought before them the brother of Jesus, who was called Christ, whose name was James, and some others; and when he had formed an accusation against them as breakers of the law, he delivered them to be stoned.*
>
> **ANTIQUITIES, 20:9:1**

The birth, life, passion, death, and resurrection of Jesus are the most important events in the history of humankind. We discovered who God is and who we are in one short lifetime. The suffering of Jesus shows us God's solidarity with man and depicts man's intrinsic worth. It shows God as a person like us, not something unseen and austere.

Jesus performed many, many spectacular miracles. Walking on water, turning water into wine, bringing the dead to life, rising from the dead Himself after predicting it, etcetera. Also, God the Father spoke to Him from the heavens out loud with dozens of witnesses at Jesus's baptism in the River Jordan and at the Transfiguration witnessed by Peter, James, and John.

Jesus asked Peter, "who do you say that I am?" Peter answered, "You are the Messiah, the Son of the living God." (Matthew 16:16).

Who do you say Jesus is?

WHO WAS JESUS CHRIST?

Jesus was such an important historical figure who has had so much impact over the last 2,000 years that it makes sense for any serious person to ask himself, *who was Jesus Christ?* Here's what history and the Bible have revealed to us.

Jesus performed hundreds of physical miracles recorded in the New Testament. Essentially, all of Galilee followed him around, seeking cures, as one might expect. Jesus's disciples also performed wondrous miracles in his name after He was gone.

For the past 2,000 years, His followers have performed thousands of physical and spiritual miracles in His name. This is not true of other religions. In other words, there are no claims of "Hindu miracles."

Jesus repeatedly claimed divinity as the Son of God. So logically, He had to be either: 1) crazy; 2) a liar; or 3) God.

> **Crazy people and liars do not perform hundreds of miracles, raise the dead, predict the future, or come back from the dead! Only Jesus did this.**

Jesus fulfilled the Scriptures, which predicted a Jewish messiah in the line of David would be born in Bethlehem. The entire Bible is about Jesus. The Old Testament can be summed up as *Jesus is coming*. The New Testament is *Jesus has come*.

If Jesus was not who He said he was, then who was He? Just some guy who performed miracles and rose from the dead?

But how do we know He really rose from the dead? The Muslims, after all, believe He never died on the cross but was only wounded or that they crucified someone else.

It is the testimony of the people who were with him. They all said He died, was laid to rest, and was resurrected on the third day. Then they went out to spread this word and, in many cases, died defending this truth.

Jesus has overwhelming credibility because of his "mighty deeds" and His words, which have the "Ring of Truth."

Here's who Jesus said he was, in his own words:

> *I am the way, the truth, and the life.*
> *I am the bread of life.*
> *I am the light of the world.*
> *I am the door of the sheep.*
> *I am the good shepherd.*
> *I am the resurrection and the life.*
> *I am the true vine. You are the branches.*

Who could say these things and then back it up? Only God Himself.

The reality and believability of Jesus does not come from one or two things. It's from an avalanche of credibility, everything from raising people from the dead to exhibiting power over nature.

37 MIRACLES OF JESUS IN CHRONOLOGICAL ORDER

1. Jesus Turns Water into Wine at the Wedding in Cana
2. Jesus Heals an Official's Son at Capernaum in Galilee
3. Jesus Drives Out an Evil Spirit from a Man in Capernaum
4. Jesus Heals Peter's Mother-in-Law Sick with Fever
5. Jesus Heals Many Sick and Oppressed at Evening
6. First Miraculous Catch of Fish on the Lake of Gennesaret
7. Jesus Cleanses a Man with Leprosy
8. Jesus Heals a Centurion's Paralyzed Servant in Capernaum
9. Jesus Heals a Paralytic Who Was Let Down from the Roof
10. Jesus Heals a Man's Withered Hand on the Sabbath
11. Jesus Raises a Widow's Son from the Dead in Nain
12. Jesus Calms a Storm on the Sea
13. Jesus Casts Demons into a Herd of Pigs
14. Jesus Heals a Woman in the Crowd with an Issue of Blood
15. Jesus Raises Jairus' Daughter Back to Life
16. Jesus Heals Two Blind Men
17. Jesus Heals a Man Who Was Unable to Speak
18. Jesus Heals an Invalid at Bethesda
19. Jesus Feeds 5,000 Plus Women and Children
20. Jesus Walks on Water

21. Jesus Heals Many Sick in Gennesaret as They Touch His Garment
22. Jesus Heals a Gentile Woman's Demon-Possessed Daughter
23. Jesus Heals a Deaf and Dumb Man
24. Jesus Feeds 4,000 Plus Women and Children
25. Jesus Heals a Blind Man at Bethsaida
26. Jesus Heals a Man Born Blind by Spitting in His Eyes
27. Jesus Heals a Boy With an Unclean Spirit
28. Miraculous Temple Tax in a Fish's Mouth
29. Jesus Heals a Blind, Mute Demoniac
30. Jesus Heals a Woman Who Had Been Crippled for 18 Years
31. Jesus Heals a Man With Dropsy on the Sabbath
32. Jesus Cleanses Ten Lepers on the Way to Jerusalem
33. Jesus Raises Lazarus from the Dead in Bethany
34. Jesus Restores Sight to Bartimaeus in Jericho
35. Jesus Withers the Fig Tree on the Road From Bethany
36. Jesus Heals a Servant's Severed Ear While He Is Being Arrested
37. The Second Miraculous Catch of Fish at the Sea of Tiberias

JESUS'S KEY MESSAGES

- Believe in Him
- Love God (because He loved you first)

- Love your neighbor
- Forgive others, and we will be forgiven
- Turn the other cheek
- Humility
- Prayer
- Repentance
- Obedience
- Keep My commandments

> *"I am the Way, the Truth, and the Life.
> No one comes to the Father except through me"*
>
> **JOHN 14:6**

This is a bold statement. Again, Jesus was either crazy, a liar, or he was God. There is no middle ground where you can say He was just a nice guy who did good deeds. Crazy liars don't raise the dead! *I'm repeating this because it is a critically important point to dwell on.*
Please dwell!

What more does Jesus have to do to make us believe?

According to John, only a fraction of these miracles were written down, which makes sense given the technology of the day. But the ones that the New Testament authors wrote down are detailed and stunning. These were his disciples who were there. If any one of these miracles is true, then the whole thing is true.

How do we comprehend all this? How do we understand that Jesus was a man and, at the same time, He was God who created the universe? This is what we call a mystery. Jesus claimed to be 100% man and 100% God simultaneously. This is possible because, with God, all things are possible since He is God.

How do we comprehend that God is also love? What does that mean? What is love? How can a person be a thing?

The fullest expression of God as love was through the Son, Jesus Christ. God created and sustains us and revealed Himself to us through Jesus.

> *And the Word became flesh and dwelt among us, and we have seen his glory, glory as of the only Son from the Father, full of grace and truth."*
>
> JOHN 1:14

Contemplate this ... Jesus's joy is complete in *us*!

> *As the Father has loved me, so have I loved you. Now remain in my love. If you keep my commandments, you will remain in my love, just as I have kept my Father's commandments and remain in his love. I have told you this so that my joy may be in you and that your joy may be complete.*
>
> JOHN 15:9-11

This passage shows how important mankind is to God which is very comforting to contemplate. Jesus revealed God to be our *Father*, which, if you think about it, is an amazing revelation because everyone can identify with it. Oh, I get it now. God is our Father ... cool!

Jesus's assertion that God was His Father first occurred in a debate about the Sabbath day of rest. Jesus claimed that it was proper for

Him to perform healings on the Sabbath because, in his words: *My Father is working until now, and I am working* (John 5:17).

In other words, although God rested on the seventh day from his work of creation, His work of preservation and ultimately of redemption was still ongoing. Moreover, Jesus associated His own ministry with the continuing work of the Father, raising the question of their relationship in a way that antagonized his fellow Jews. As the Gospel records:

> *That was why the Jews were seeking all the more to kill him, because not only was he breaking the Sabbath, but he was even calling God his own Father, making himself equal with God.*
>
> **JOHN 5:18**

But as John described in this most beautiful way, Jesus *was* equal with God. Jesus is the *Word of God*.

> *In the beginning was the Word: The Word was with God and the Word was God.*
>
> *He was with God in the beginning.*
>
> *Through him all things came into being, not one thing came into being except through him.*
>
> *What has come into being in him was life, life that was the light of men; and light shines in darkness, and darkness could not overpower it.*
>
> **JOHN 1:1-5**

How did Christianity spread from a handful of Jesus's disciples in a tiny outpost of the Roman empire? The Jews had been waiting for a Messiah for thousands of years, and Jesus came and said, "I am He." But how did it spread from there?

Jesus sent out His disciples two by two to other countries. But if you think about it, these countries were not Jewish by any means—people in these countries spoke a different language, and were generally hostile. How did these two guys convert large sections of the civilized world? These countries weren't even looking for a Messiah.

It is because they spoke with authority and authenticity—but also because they *were working miracles just as Jesus had.*

So, the fact that Christianity spread throughout the world like it did bears witness to the reality that Jesus existed, who He was, and the clear superiority of the Christian worldview.

CHAPTER 9

REVIEW: EXISTENCE OF GOD

Let's pause for a second and recap what we've covered so far:
Simply put, we know there is a God because, by scientific principle, matter and energy cannot create themselves. By logic, there has to be a Principal Cause.

The universe is ordered. Richard Feynman, a Nobel Prize winner for quantum electrodynamics, said, "Why nature is mathematical is a mystery ... the fact that there are rules at all is a kind of miracle."

The development of organic life from inorganic matter is manifestly impossible. A rock could never turn into a fish through evolution. But is this what atheists believe?

Scientists have calculated the odds of one living protein coming into existence by chance are 10 with 67 zeroes to 1. In other words, it is mathematically impossible. But it did.

My son Robbie emailed me something he found called *The Math of God*. Here is an excerpt:

> Astronomer Hoyle and his colleague concluded that there is only one chance in 10 [to the power] 40,000 that even

a single enzyme could have evolved by random processes, a figure that is "statistically impossible." It would require more attempts to form one enzyme than there are atoms in all the stars in all the known galaxies. This statistic was not arrived at by guessing but by computations based on the necessary components of enzymes.

Therefore, according to Hoyle and colleague—previously non-theists—spontaneous generation is impossible, requiring a miracle. "Because of the impossibility of the chance formation and development of life anywhere in the universe," and since the universe is not eternal, they have abandoned the steady state theory Hoyle helped formulate years ago.

Scientists have calculated that if the Big Bang had caused the universe's rate of expansion to be 1 part in 100 thousand trillion slower or faster, the universe would have either re-collapsed or been too strong to form stars or planets. The same applies to the strong nuclear force that holds protons and neutrons together. If any different, heavier elements like carbon could not have formed

In other words, a pattern is seen as science makes more discoveries. The universe and the Earth are uniquely designed to support human life. Not only are we not an accident of nature, man appears to be the reason for all existence. In our culture, the inference of the term "Mother Nature" often is "Everything just happened by itself."

Again, there is no way this all happened by itself.

Most people—even the poor and illiterate—understand this intuitively, but many intellectuals don't.

The existence of God, angels, the spiritual world, the afterlife, demons, and ghosts have been a basic belief of man for thousands of years. The occasional appearance of ghosts confirms this.

I like this one: If someone found a camera on Mars, would they assume somebody left it there, or would it just evolve by itself? Same with the universe—its laws and order are infinitely more complex than a camera. Did it just happen by itself?

Then you've got the miracles (more to come on this!)

Without God, there is no Hope. Nothingness constantly looms over every man, for "without Christ's resurrection, only one alternative remains: nothingness" (*The Risen Christ*, Luigi Giussani).

Also, even the devil believes in God.

For there not to be a God, it means logically that everything we see happened by itself, and there was no First Mover, no guiding hand, no nothing to help it along. This is doubtful, as I have shown.

Even if you still say, "No, Bob, I think everything *did* just happen by itself," there's still the problem of the intricate laws of nature. The universe operates by rules. How did they get there? Water boils at 100° C. Why? These laws can't have invented themselves. Even if you say they are intrinsic to nature, there's no reason why they are ordered as such.

The DNA code that runs our bodies is nothing more than a highly complex computer software program. It's like saying the first iPhone just came into existence by itself. No, it had to have a designer, a programmer by logic.

Then, there is the simple and understandable concept that order can only come from order, and disorder comes from disorder.

Jesus himself makes a splendid case for the existence of God. He identified Himself as God and then proceeded to do hundreds of

God-like actions and ultimately predicted he would be tortured, killed, and raised up on the third day. And then that happened.

Finally if you're not convinced by any of these five things: 1) the "Math of God" that everything could not have happened by itself; 2) the intricate laws of nature that couldn't have invented themselves; 3) our highly complex DNA programming which by logic had to have a programmer; 4) the simple concept that order cannot come from disorder without a guiding hand; and 5) Jesus Himself who actually said he was God and backed it up every way imaginable, we are now face-to-face with Pascal's Wager. Why? **Because you realize that you don't know** and there's a *possibility* that it may all be true, in which case it is only sensible to believe and live your life as such. Why would you take the chance?

PART 2

FROM REASON TO FAITH

CHAPTER 10

GOING DEEPER: FAITH

So dear readers, if Jesus did all these things, He was God; therefore, there is a God. If He came down here, literally walked on water, and raised the dead, this becomes a spectacular reason to believe in God.

But how do we know this is not some fairy tale or Aesop's fable? Well, we do measure time from when Jesus was born, so He probably was a real person. I don't think too many myths have that kind of influence on the world. It's interesting to note that the Gregorian calendar that we measure time with today is from the sixteenth century, compiled by the Jesuits.

Belief in Jesus as the Son of God caused thousands to become martyrs for the faith. Then you have the many, many miracles that have been done in his name over the past 2,000 years. The New Testament has detailed accounts of the life of Jesus and what He did, the miracles He performed, and what His disciples did after He left. Many non-biblical sources support Jesus's existence, including letters from the Church Fathers who knew Him and His apostles. They were one person removed from knowing Jesus personally.

Finally, if you're still not believing through reason because everything couldn't happen by itself, and the laws of nature couldn't create themselves, and you think Pascal's Wager doesn't make sense, I beg you to ask yourself... why? Why don't you believe?

Hopefully, it's not "it will inconvenience my lifestyle and force me to do things I do not want to do and infringe on my freedoms. I want to make the rules because I can determine right and wrong for me."

Again, this is playing fast and loose with your most valuable possession—your soul—and fast and loose with eternity. It is the Original Sin of the Garden of Eden.

When we were on our Holy Land trip in 2008, we met Fr. Eamon Kelly, and he took us to the Shroud of Turin exhibit near the Notre Dame hotel. One thing that really struck me is that he said faith begins with obedience. I hadn't thought of it that way, but it does if you think about it. This begs another question—if faith is rooted in obedience, is lack of faith rooted in disobedience?

It is an important question that we should ask ourselves. Is our position on the existence of God based upon us being a rebel? It's often good to rebel in this world, but if there is a God, we can all agree that we should not rebel against Him. Many of us were taught that God exists by our parents or in school. I look upon that as a gift. For those of us who were instructed about God, it's certainly a rebellion against that teaching if we don't believe. Faith does *begin* with obedience. And lack of faith *is* rooted in disobedience.

If you start from the position that there is no God, you are not being obedient to logic because *you really don't know.* The only position you could take logically is that you don't know whether there is a God or not, which would make you an agnostic but not an atheist.

Faith begins with reason, and moreover, it *must* begin with reason.

It is illogical to believe anything without reason. If someone says I believe the Earth is flat, they must give reasons, which should be verifiable and compelling. From the logic in this discussion, either you are a rebel against God if deep down you believe from what you were taught that there is a God, or you are a true agnostic on whether there is a God or not. You say you don't know—which implies that you could know if you had enough knowledge one way or the other. So, the reason you don't have faith could be you don't have enough knowledge. Hopefully I am helping providing that knowledge here.

Faith starts with reason and ends in faith. Reason leads you 99% there. But as the old saying goes, you can lead a horse to water, but you can't make him drink!

We know that the vast majority of people who have ever existed believed in some type of god, but you say you know there is none? This is the position of a rebel for sure!

I think all of us, to some extent, hide from God—just as Adam and Eve did in the garden after they ate the forbidden fruit. God knows this is normal. He's not trying to rub our face in it. He wants us to understand the truth and to make incremental changes—baby steps toward him.

If it's true that God created man and then rescued him by giving himself up to be tortured by man, what does that say about God, and what does that say about man? It speaks of God's intrinsic love for man and the intrinsic value of man who must be worth it in God's eyes.

For an atheist, neither one is true. There is no God, so there is no notion of the intrinsic value of man. He's just one of the more intelligent animals that happened to pop up on the planet. You can see how this leads to a completely different worldview between the theist and non-theist, leading to opposite opinions on the day's issues.

Faith is an adventure. It's a hero's journey. You get out of your comfort zone. God Himself calls forth the journey and calls us out of our comfortable domesticity.

It's a question of whose team do you want to be on. Do you really want to be against God? With eternity hanging in the balance? In the face of Pascal's Wager?

At this point, let's say you are thinking, "Okay, Bob, you convinced me! I will try to believe in God, and I don't want to be stupid about Pascal's Wager. And you never know, maybe there is a God."

But now I have more bad news. Your problem now is you can't be halfway on this or lukewarm.

> *But since you are like lukewarm water, neither hot nor cold, I will spit you out of my mouth!*
>
> **REVELATION 3:16**

Well, that's a bit sobering ...

You can't be in the middle, either. Jesus said either *you're with me,* or *you're against me.*

> *Christianity, if false, is of no importance, and if true, of infinite importance. The only thing it cannot be is moderately important.*
>
> **C.S. LEWIS**

These words have the ring of truth, do they not? Quotes like this are the reason C.S. Lewis is C.S. Lewis.

If you believe in God, it changes the way you look at your life. Earthly goals, while good and important, become secondary to the real goal and the reason we are here. We are here to obtain everlasting salvation, everlasting happiness and joy.

So, dear reader, who are you going to hitch your wagon to? What's it going to say on your casket? Where does your hope lie?

DOES FAITH MATTER? CAN'T WE JUST LIVE GOOD LIVES?

We are bound by man's innate dignity to seek the truth, and once we find it, to adhere to it and live it. Man is drawn to the truth by his own nature, by his own freedom. God won't force it on us.

Man must always listen to his conscience no matter what it tells him. However, it is not permissible to indulge in error without seeking the truth. The essential usefulness of faith is that man achieves the good of his rational nature through faith. We say, ultimately, only God can save man, but he expects man to cooperate. The fact that man can cooperate with God determines his authentic greatness.

Pope John Paul II

John Paul II also said, "Without the Gospel, we can easily find ourselves far from the truth about man. Who is man if the Son took on human nature? Who must man be if the Son pays the supreme price for his dignity? On the heels of faith comes humility. Faith is recognizing the truth of who God is and who we are. The more we understand this, the more we start to get on our knees. Our ego naturally recedes as we stand before our Maker in awe. We begin to see that everything we have in our life is a gift, and every gift has been given to us gratuitously. This is the ultimate recognition of reality."

The Apostle's Creed is a relatively short prayer summarizing everything Christians believe. If you are struggling with your faith or even belief in God, this prayer is simple and powerful:

> *I believe in God,*
> *the Father almighty,*
> *Creator of heaven and Earth,*
> *and in Jesus Christ, his only Son, our Lord,*
> *who was conceived by the Holy Spirit,*
> *born of the Virgin Mary,*
> *suffered under Pontius Pilate,*
> *was crucified, died, and was buried;*
> *he descended into hell;*
> *on the third day, he rose again from the dead;*
> *he ascended into heaven,*
> *and is seated at the right hand of God the Father almighty;*
> *from there, he will come to judge the living and the dead.*
> *I believe in the Holy Spirit,*
> *the holy catholic* Church,*
> *the communion of saints,*
> *the forgiveness of sins,*
> *the resurrection of the body,*
> *and life everlasting.*
> *Amen.*

---

* Note that the word catholic is small c, meaning universality.

CHAPTER 11

WHAT IF YOU WERE GOD?

God created the entire universe, the physical laws, the planets, and stars, and He created the animals, plants, angels, and human beings. He gave free will only to the angels and humans, and both rebelled against Him immediately. God probably had complete foreknowledge of this, but I would think this had to disappoint Him.

Ask yourself: What if you were God? What would you do if everybody rebelled against you? Would you be angry?

Here's a better question: If you were God, would you be authentic? Or would you be kind of a con man god where you created everybody and everything, but then just let it all ride through time and get your kicks out of people's misery?

Do you think someone who could make the universe, create rainbows and mountains and animals and intricate laws of nature and people who love each other ... do you think someone who could do that would be inauthentic? Do you think he would be a bad guy? Do you think he would create billions of people just to torture them for his amusement? Because that's what you think if you don't trust God. You believe that God is either uncaring or really doesn't get it or is just stupid.

But how could the Creator of the universe be stupid or devious or selfish or even human? He would have to be above that, right? He would have to be a lot better than you or me!

God created the angels first, and apparently, there were millions of them. From Scripture, we know that many of them, perhaps one-third by some estimates, rebelled and turned against God, upset about the whole idea of man's creation, composed of a mortal body with an angel-like spirit.

It seems like God was angry about this and cast them into hell. But we don't talk much about how God felt about this. If it were you or me, we'd be very hurt, and I believe God was very hurt as well. You might say, how can a vast and powerful God be hurt? But we know from Christian teaching that God is offended by our sins, and we know for sure that Jesus was hurt in every imaginable way in His persecution, torture, and death while on Earth.

If God is a person, He must have feelings, and if we think about it, that's where our feelings come from too. We are made in *the image and likeness of God*. How could a God with no feelings make humans with feelings?

Today, aren't many of us rebelling against God like the angels did? As God looks down upon His creation of 8 billion people at any given moment, how many of them are even thinking about Him? How many of them appreciate what He has done in creating and sustaining us and what Jesus did to save us from certain destruction to eternal joy?

God sees people break the Ten Commandments left and right. When we rebel against our human fathers, there are consequences. Similarly, if we rebel against God, there are consequences. This must be so for God to be authentic. The consequence is that we lose some of the protections that we had. Our dad takes away the car keys or cuts off our allowance. This explains the hardship we face in life. It is our doing, not God's doing.

To sin against God is no small thing. It is a rejection of our Creator and his laws. Therefore, the consequences must be big, and that is what we see in the world today. That's also why it took a big thing, God himself taking the form of man, to offset this rebellion and to make it right.

Authentic in this context means the purpose of God is (must be) for man. By the way, Jesus was surely authentic! I doubt anyone can argue that.

Since everyone was created in the image and likeness of God, we all have implanted in us a desire for truth. In a sense, there is really no such thing as atheism. People just substitute themselves as God. Today's pluralism suggests we let everyone define their own good. It's a new kind of atheism, where Man is the source of truth, not God.

People know authenticity when they see it. Jesus's disciples must have had it.

Christ is the fullness of revelation of man as well as God. He is the answer to the question that is every human life. Man is a mystery to himself.

God takes a lot of abuse. Makes you wonder why.

Also, God restricts Himself... would we?

God is obviously all-powerful and all-knowing. I believe that God is also all-loving and all-just. But through reason we also know that God intentionally restricts His own power and influence. He respects His agreements with all His creatures. That is the reason there is so much misery in the world. He gives the devil some rope to do his thing. Again, this is a temporary thing. He uses Satan to test us. **He wants to know whose side we are on.**

John Paul II said, "God's gift of rationality and free will to humankind made Him subject to man's judgment. The history of salvation is also the history of man's continual judgment of God. It also shows the judgment of man and God by the devil" (see Job 1:6-22).

Why should we trust God? Well, for starters, would we trust ourselves if we were God? Maybe not, but we can be sure that God is much better than we would be. The other reason to trust God is that he has *proven Himself* with the incarnation of Jesus Christ, who overcame death. He predicted that He would rise on the third day, and He did.

Trusting God doesn't mean that we are entirely passive. We take medicine when we're sick, buckle our seatbelts in our cars, and are cautious with our affairs. We should aim to trust God with the outcome.

Some people misinterpret this and think since we trust God, we can sit back and wait for Him to take care of it. God expects us to use the brain He gave us. We can pray for miracles, but we cannot presume one. That would put God to the test, which is not good. We trust God — not necessarily with the hope that we'll get exactly what we want right now — but with the *ultimate outcome*.

Suppose a family member has a terrible tragedy or early death, but ultimately, we end up living with that person in eternal bliss. In that case, did we not get what we asked for when we prayed? Jesus said, "You will not look back."

This is further complicated because of the influence of Satan, who was an angel and rebelled against God. He also suffered enormous consequences. God is a loving God who has prepared for us a place that "eyes have not seen nor ears heard" (from St. Paul), but he requires certain things of us as His creatures.

Our idea of a tragedy is if we die when we're 25 instead of 85. That's not how God sees it. His idea of a tragedy is if we reject Him and go to hell. We are very concerned with the length and physical and emotional quality of our lives. God looks at it differently in the framework of eternity.

Every day is one more gift, an opportunity to seek God. That's what He wants—for us to seek him, ask, and knock.

God doesn't look at things the way we do, although he understands why we see things the way we do. He sometimes doesn't seem as concerned about our problems, which are colossal to us, because He sees the bigger and more important picture. He is concerned about our everlasting salvation, whereas we're concerned about next week!

Consider this: **life = short, eternity = really, really, really long!**

We're going to be alive for a short period of time, and then we're going to be dead for a *very* long, infinite period of time. So, which one should we be focused on? Which one *do* we focus on?

God is trying to get our attention without turning us into puppets. If you could make a deal with God where He would say you will undergo 10 minutes of reasonably intense pain and disappointment, but in exchange, He would provide you with 70 years of bliss and good fortune—isn't that a pretty good deal?

That's the deal God is making with us. Only it's much, much better than that. The ratio of 70 years to 10 minutes is nothing compared to when we are talking about our short lives on Earth versus eternity. Plus, our life on Earth has many great and rewarding moments. And the more we focus on the end goal of eternal life with our Creator and Lord, the better and easier it gets down here during our "10 minutes."

Separated. This state is not the way God intended it to be. **Even if YOU were God, would you not have a plan?** What would be your end game?

God's end game is to be with us in paradise. If you don't believe in God, you probably don't believe in Bible Scriptures, but just the same, consider this:

The book of Revelation reveals God's plan:

> *I heard a loud voice from the throne saying*
> *"Behold, God's dwelling is with the human race.*
> *He will dwell with them and they will be his people*
> *and God himself will always be with them as their God.*
> *He will wipe every tear from their eyes,*
> *and there shall be no more death or mourning,*
> *wailing or pain,*
> *for the old order has passed away."*

Oh! So that's it?

God's dwelling is with the human race. We are God's creation, and He wants to live with us as opposed to now when we are separated. It will be God, the angels, and us living in eternity. Sounds okay, no? We are vitally important to God's plan. We will be in His presence and share His life in all its unfathomable splendor, mystery, and universal love.

The God who created everything we see wants to be our friend and wants us to learn to love like He does. God is not the Absolute, which remains outside the world, indifferent to man's suffering. No, He is with us, sharing in man's lot and participating in his destiny. God, besides omnipotence is wisdom and love and desires to justify Himself to mankind.

God places Himself on the side of man, *in a radical way.*

Consider the fact that Jesus could have come to Earth in many ways. He could have just appeared on the scene as God speaking to man. But he became man — a little baby growing up just as we all do. He's one of us!

We were originally destined to be protected in the Garden of Eden. That was the way God meant it to be. The hardship, disease, and accidents came after we broke God's trust and turned against him, misusing His gift of free will. We lost some, but not all, of God's protection. Okay, you can call it a punishment, but it's more like when we punish our children — is it not for their own good?

We are only partially cut off from God; some people always feel connected. We are all flawed from birth, and the reasons that we reject truth stem from pride, ignorance, and laziness. But as we gain the truth and take it to heart, the pride, ignorance, and laziness start to melt away.

God is not looking for ways to condemn us. He's looking for ways to save us. He is not looking to say, "Gotcha!" That wouldn't make any sense even if you were God. Why would you create a child and prepare a place to spend eternity and then arbitrarily send him to everlasting damnation? The real God can't be less moral than us, less loving.

He is jealous of His dignity and could not permit Himself to be outdone by His creature on the score of fidelity and generosity.

Fr. Charles Armingon

SATAN

It's probably not a good idea to dwell a lot on what if you were Satan. But consider just for an instant that you rebelled against God and were cast into hell forever. Your reaction must be that you hate God. You would want to subvert anything God is doing, and to do that; you have to lie. Because God is about truth, and deep down you probably realize this, and if you're going to subvert God, you must lie, lie, lie.

So, you are Captain Opposite. What's good is bad and what's bad is good. Consequently, the first thing you do is try to convince people that God does not even exist. Or if you already believe He exists, God is against you. This is what the devil is trying to get you to think every day. Don't let him do it to you.

We can readily see Satan's influence in our Captain Opposite culture today. The second thing he tries to do is convince us that he does not exist. This lie has even entered the churches were many priests and pastors rarely talk about these things. Satan is the master of lies and is very skilled in his propaganda. Recommended reading on this topic: *The Screwtape Letters* by C.S. Lewis is an excellent and entertaining source to understand how the devil works.

CHAPTER 12

BARRIERS TO BELIEF

I think it is safe to say that since the beginning of humankind, most people have believed in God. Even the pagans have their gods. The fact is that most people innately understand that creation must have a Creator. Man is hardwired to believe in God, and if we don't, we will substitute something else—money, health, drugs, career, or ourselves.

There are three main reasons why people doubt the existence of God:

1. **Pain**—They do not believe a loving God would allow so much pain and suffering.
2. **Hiddenness**—He is hidden. Out of sight, out of mind.
3. **Busyness**—We are busy in our daily lives, and deep down, we're afraid of changing our lives.

We must get past the barriers, or every time there's a tragedy or we can't feel God's presence, we go, "Oops, guess there's no God!"

THE PROBLEM OF PAIN

God created us to live in communion with Him in paradise. We turned away from God, not the other way around. Sin had consequences.

When we cut ourselves off from God, we lost part of His protection in this world. We must struggle and endure pain.

Although it often seems long, the pain we endure in this lifetime is short and the promise of salvation is infinite and great. Just like the end of a race—it is all worth it if you win. Right?

Would you endure 10 seconds of pain for 1,000 years of happiness? Or 10 years of pain for 100,000 years of bliss? Infinity is much longer than that!

Jesus said, "On that day, you will not ask me any questions." (John 16:23) This means to me heaven will be so good we won't look back.

But why do some people seem to have much more pain and hardship than others? We don't know. Maybe our pain helps others to deal with their pain or get to heaven if we accept it and still trust God. We are all in this together, and clearly this is what God wants—for us to live our lives by helping others along the way.

Also, we do not understand everything. God's mind is so far above our mind we can never fully know it. For God, "a day is like 1,000 years and 1,000 years like a day."

Unless understood in a Christian sense, pain is meaningless. Pain is a shared suffering with Christ.

The cross is proof of God's solidarity with man in its suffering.

Pope John Paul II

Through the hardships of life, we do experience much suffering. But our attitude toward it is very important. Suppose we gripe and grouse and go to great lengths to avoid even minor discomfort. In that case, we are wasting a great opportunity to unite and align our pain with the sufferings of Christ. It brings great meaning to something that is otherwise totally pointless. Just as Jesus sided with us in a radical way, we side with Him.

My wife and I were watching the television series *1883*, which is about settlers trying to travel west in America in the nineteenth century. We were struck by the incredible hardships they faced with attacks by bandits, drownings trying to cross rivers, rattlesnakes, tornadoes, Indians, children dying of smallpox, etcetera. The reason they took this journey is because they had already faced incredible oppression in their native European countries. They must have felt completely abandoned by God.

Clearly, some people have easier times than others. Some people live long lives, and some people die as children. So, either there is no God at all, or we're looking at it the wrong way.

We are looking at it the wrong way. God is not so interested as we are in what happens to us in this world; He is interested in what happens to us in the next world.

When they asked Jesus about this, what did He say? He said the last shall be first and the first last. Wow! That provides an entirely different outlook, doesn't it?

I believe I have had a relatively easy time growing up in this beautiful country with wonderful parents and family. I've had an exciting career and so far, I am living a pretty long time with general good health. Strangely, I find it comforting that the people less fortunate than me are going to the front of the line in the next world. That's fine with me just so I'm in there somewhere!

But we must remember, we are being tested.

We should look at heaven with God as our home and Earth as our temporary exile. It is a test, and sometimes a difficult test to determine if we are a friend to God or not.

Does it seem right that even though we messed up big time (sin) and Jesus totally bailed us out by being tortured and killed, we just spend our lives immersed in secular concerns and personal comfort?

He wants us to freely choose Him, and there needs to be a certain amount of hardship and chaos or we just won't do it. If we're already in Utopia, why would we seek anything else?

But to freely choose Him, we must have free will. If we have free will, it means we can reject Him, too. He has shown through the works of Jesus that He is authentic and trying to cut us slack in every way imaginable. Still, ultimately, it's on us—because God refuses to be our puppeteer.

THE PROBLEM OF HIDDENNESS

We often wonder why God doesn't just show Himself, come down here, perform wondrous miracles and acts, explain who He is, who we are, how we are to live our lives, and what is in store for us after we die.

Well, He did! Jesus Christ performed literally thousands of miracles—to the point where nearly the entire population of Galilee followed Him around wherever He went. He fulfilled the Scriptures, suffered, died for our sins, founded a Church and commanded His disciples to spread the word over the entire Earth.

For those struggling to believe—is there anything God could do to make you believe He exists? How about creating the universe out of nothing? Pretty good trick, isn't it? What about coming down as a human, performing miracles, raising the dead, predicting that He would die but rise from the dead in three days—and then actually do it? How about predicting and allowing his followers to perform many miracles themselves? Is there anything else you could think of?

Okay, you might say, but that was 2,000 years ago. Why has He been so hidden since then?

Clearly, God wants us to choose Him freely with our free will. If He made a miracle in the sky every day, we would be more or less forced to believe and obey. Our free will would be eroded, and we would be more like puppets.

That said, He has left us many miracles and signs as reminders that He is still with us as promised.

Some people just can't imagine that there is a God because it seems so fantastic and unreal. We are used to things we can touch, taste, hear, and see. People sometimes think we're supposed to believe in a white-bearded old man in the sky who determines whether we go to heaven with angels and harps or hell with demons and fire. To some, this is no different than the tooth fairy (apologies to anyone reading this who believes in the tooth fairy!).

But pause and think about all the things we routinely believe in that we can't see. All the dimensions of the light spectrum, of which we can only see a small part, are nevertheless there. Radio waves, Wi-Fi, and all sorts of technology shooting around us that we can't see or fully understand have a profound impact on our lives. We can't see thoughts, but we know people are having them.

Plus, there is ample evidence of the existence of the spiritual world. Ghosts, for instance, have been part of human culture for thousands of years. This belief is a fundamental tenet for man. And many people have had profound spiritual experiences that completely changed their lives.

Then you have the records of near-death experiences, which is where science apparently meets the outskirts of the spiritual world. There are many records of people dying on the operating table, floating above their bodies, and later being able to describe the room and everything that occurred in great detail. I can recommend a good book on the subject, *After* by Dr. Bruce Greyson of the University of Virginia.

Remember that the spiritual world came first. If there is a Creator, by definition it's from outside the physical world, right? Matter cannot make itself. This proves (unless everything just happened by itself!) that there is an intelligent being outside of the physical world, which came later in the order of creation.

And the spiritual world operates by different rules. It is reality—much more so than the physical world. It is the realm where God exists, the angels, and all the departed souls from this world. It's where creation came from.

You may have a problem with the idea of the spiritual world, but you should know that some of the angels had a big problem with the concept of the physical world and the creation of man! They thought it was ridiculous, so they broke away from God, and He let them go, respecting their free will. That's where we got the devils and demons who tried to subvert God's plan of creation—using their gift of free will.

We know all this through reason, not faith. We use reason that there had to be a first mover that created the physical world, which logically had to be a supreme entity in a non-physical realm.

God created the spiritual and physical worlds and combined them to make humankind. The spiritual world is manifested in the physical world through creation, especially that of man. The physical world is permeated by the spiritual.

Many people have seen signs and wonders evidencing the existence of God, angels, saints, the afterlife, and spiritual world. But it is comforting to know what Jesus said to Saint Thomas, the doubting

Thomas who said he would not believe that Jesus had resurrected until he put his hands in His wounds. He did so, and he did believe but Jesus said, "Blessed are those who have believed and not seen." This is an opportunity for the vast majority of us to be blessed!

BUSYNESS AND THE PROBLEM DEEP DOWN

There is one more reason people doubt. Expressing a belief system carries with it an implied set of standards and rules. Thomas Merton said people don't convert because deep down they know they will have to change their lives. Many people simply don't want those restrictions placed on them.

French philosopher and writer Albert Camus had an interesting way of looking at this idea:

> *Everyone wants the happy life.*
> *Some men like to deceive, but nobody*
>   *wants to be deceived.*
> *All men would rather have joy in truth than*
>   *joy in falsity.*
> *Joy in truth is the happy life*
> *Why then does truth beget hatred?*
>   *It is because men want to love some other thing and they want that to be the truth and since they don't want to be deceived, they convince themselves they are not deceived.*
>   *Therefore, they hate the truth for the sake of the thing that they love. They hate the truth because it accuses them. They are walking in a different Kingdom, slaves to the "father of lies" who has blinded them to the truth.*

When you don't want to believe, you won't believe. Jesus performed many miracles in His day and many of the people who witnessed them still didn't believe—especially the Jewish clergy at the time. They would get on Jesus's case for healing the sick on Sundays! How messed up is that?

But they had a reason to not believe, because what Jesus was saying and doing would rock their world. It would rock their religious authority and power which they clung to.

It's the same now. People see what they want to see. There are miracles and reports of miracles if you simply look for them.

CHAPTER 13

MIRACLES, MIRACLES, AND MY TEMPUR-PEDIC MIRACLE

A survey from the Pew Forum on Religion & Public Life showed that a vast majority of Americans, nearly 80%, believe in miracles. The results are from a wider study, "Religion Among the Millennials."

The survey shows that people of faith are more likely to believe in miracles, but the nonbelievers are also increasingly believing in miracles, which is nonsensical because how can you believe in miracles but not believe in the only One who could possibly do miracles, which is God?

It seems only the most ardent atheist does not believe in miracles. So, if you believe in miracles but not in God, I think it really means that you *do* believe in God on some level. And if you fit in this category, you should develop that belief for all the reasons stated in this book.

It has always struck me that Christians say, "Praise God" or "Thank you Lord!" if something good happens. But if something bad happens, they don't blame God. If you attribute your good fortune to God, what about life's bad things? It all came from Him, right? If there is a natural disaster where almost everybody gets wiped out, but some people survive, Christians will see the survivors as a miracle and praise God. But those who are nonbelievers or weak in their faith will either blame God or point to it as evidence that there is no God. I am going to walk you through why this is the case.

Christians believe in God because they know everything could not have happened by itself, and they were taught this as children or discovered it on their own. They believe in the promise of salvation from Jesus Christ and know that what happens on this Earth, however disappointing, will be made right in eternity. They trust that God will make all things right and realize the difficulties we face on Earth are often of our own making given the flawed nature of mankind. It is because they have a different fundamental *worldview* of who we are and how we got here.

There have been so many astounding and countless miracles performed in the name of Jesus over the last 2,000 years that it would take whole libraries to account for them all. Here are just a few:

- The many uncorrupted bodies of saints, most of which are in Europe. People who died and 100 years later were dug up and found to be in the same state when they died. They didn't decompose. Many are hundreds of years old and on display in churches.

- The stigmata on many holy men and women since the first one St. Francis of Assisi in 1224. The stigmata is the permanent or semipermanent appearance of the wounds of Christ on an individual. According to various sources, there are about 25 such people in the world at any given time. I know one of them personally; he stayed at our house and is clearly legitimate.

- The first apparition of the Blessed Virgin Mary (known to Protestants as Mother Mary) was to St. Gregory in 243 AD There have been many hundreds since.

- Our Lady of Guadalupe in Mexico. Mary appeared to Juan Diego in 1531, and her image miraculously appeared on his cloak. The cloak has not deteriorated in 500 years, and there is no scientific explanation for how the image appears on the cloak. Under a microscope, it appears to float on the surface. Our Lady of Guadalupe is completely beyond scientific explanation.

- Our Lady of Fatima appeared to three shepherd children on the 13th day of 6 consecutive months in 1917. She promised a miracle to occur on October 13. A crowd of 70,000 assembled and witnessed the "Miracle of the Sun" where the sun changed colors, rotated like a fire wheel, and appeared to fall from the sky.

- Thousands of miraculous healings are associated with the saints or holy places like Fatima or Lourdes.

- Countless reports of faith healings from Christian charismatic groups.

- Through prayer and laying of hands, many thousands have changed their lives spiritually, emotionally, and physically and have found peace on Earth.

- There have been many Eucharistic miracles where the Communion host at Mass started bleeding. The most famous was Lanciano, Italy, in the eighth century where the host turned to flesh and blood. It is still on display today at the Church of St. Francis in Lanciano.

I find the apparitions of Mary to be particularly interesting. These have been consistent in almost every corner of the world for more than 1,700 years and have been associated with many miracles. Why would God choose Mary? Why not just have Jesus appear or Peter or Paul or Moses?

It's because Jesus named Mary as the mother of all of us at the foot of the cross. Mary has a position of honor among humans as the mother of Jesus. Jesus as a Jew was bound by the commandment *Honor Thy Father and Thy Mother,* and He does this perfectly.

MY MIRACLE STORY

My background is in racehorses, and I have been involved in the thoroughbred horse industry since I left college. When I was 40 years old, the horse business I depended upon went into a severe recession. I had two little kids, no job, two mortgages (since we moved and couldn't sell our house), and I was $1 million in debt. I owed everybody in town.

I did not know what to do, so I fell back on my Catholic upbringing and started attending Mass in the mornings. I rolled up my sleeves, and I went to church. I prayed that God would show me a way to provide for my family. I started to view any opportunity that came my way as a possible answer to my prayer. I started some businesses that either failed or needed to generate more to support us.

But then, a miracle happened. Through my French horse trainer, I met a Swedish horse chiropractor, who knew a Swedish horseman, Mikael Magnusson, who also claimed to make the world's greatest mattress.

I flew to Stockholm to meet Mikael and slept on the mattress at his home. I realized that this was an extraordinary product. I told Mikael I was interested, and he said, "Well, we're looking to go worldwide. Go back home and write me a marketing plan, and we will see."

And the rest is history. Eleven years later, I was CEO of a billion-dollar company on the New York Stock Exchange. There is no doubt in my mind that this was an answer to my prayer. I was thoroughly committed to the racehorse industry, knew nothing about mattresses, and had no background in selling or marketing consumer goods. But with God all things are possible; when He gives, He gives abundantly.

I was just looking for a way to make a living!

CHAPTER 14

GOD MAKES DEALS WITH HIS PEOPLE

God established many covenants with Man as he revealed Himself over time. A "covenant" is a *contract that binds two parties, with each doing their part.* It's a two-way contract. God's covenants were all rooted in His unconditional love, mercy, protection, and friendship towards His people.

1. Covenant with Noah: God established a covenant with Noah and his descendants never again to flood the Earth, destroying all life (Genesis 9:9). This covenant is established with all of humanity. Humanity is tasked with fulfilling seven commandments (do not worship idols, do not curse God, establish courts of justice, do not commit murder, do not commit sexual immorality, do not steal, do not eat flesh torn from a living animal).

2. Covenant with Abraham: God established a covenant with Abraham that he would make a great nation of his descendants through which the whole world will be blessed

(Genesis 12:1-3). On his part, Abraham had to leave the land of his youth and enter into the land promised to him. Abraham and his descendants also were required to circumcise all male descendants.

3. Covenant with Moses: God established a covenant with Moses (Exodus 19–24) in which the Jewish people were freed from slavery and became God's special possession. Not only will they be blessed, but God will claim them as his very own. The Mosaic covenant has 613 commandments, which the Jewish people must fulfill to benefit from the covenant.

4. Covenant with David: God established a covenant with David that the Messiah would come from David's descendants (2 Samuel 7). This covenant did not task the Jewish people or Gentiles with any new commandments to fulfill.

5. The New Covenant: God promised to establish a new covenant with us through the prophet Jeremiah (Jeremiah 31:31-34), which was then fulfilled in Jesus (Luke 22:20). This covenant does away with the legal requirements of commandments and replaces them with a desire of the heart to do the will of God. This covenant is with all humanity.

This last covenant is the secret to life and could not be more beautiful — **the desire of the heart to do the will of God.**

CHAPTER 15

WHY ARE WE HERE? (HINT: IT'S A TEST)

We don't really know why God created us. It makes some sense He would want to share his life with others. But if you think it through, life is really *a test* to see if we are with our Creator or against Him. If you are not with Him, you are against Him. He wants us to believe more than anything else, *even more than our actions.*

If this wasn't a test, why else would we be here? To entertain the gods? If we didn't appear randomly, then the reason we are here can't be random either.

But what about the Garden of Eden? Before there was sin, what was the purpose of humankind? It was the same. The whole Garden of Eden story of Adam and Eve is about a test of obedience and trust and God had to know that we would use our free will to flunk it.

God wanted to know way back then if His humans were going to side with Him or with the devil who broke away from his Creator. It's the same today: heaven is where God resides, hell is where the devil resides, and God is testing us to see whose side we are on.

Why are we here? To do God's will. To return to our Creator. It's pretty simple.

The Catechism of the Catholic Church says we are here *to know love and serve God.* This must come first. It doesn't mean we can't have other interests, other things in our lives. It just means that we can't put God in the back of the bus. If we do that, we run into trouble in life.

"I am the Lord thy God, thou shalt not have strange gods before me." This is the First Commandment and it's the first commandment we all break.

We are exiled here on Earth. St. Therese of Lisieux said, "The world is our ship and not our home." If you think about it, doesn't that seem right? Sure, this world can be a wonderful place, but there's tremendous hardship, pain, struggle, and torment in the world too. Is it not somewhere in our DNA — perhaps buried in many of us — that understands that this is not all there is and that there is a better place for us?

We should look at heaven with God as our home and Earth as our temporary exile. Life is a test, and sometimes a difficult test, to determine if we are a friend of God or not.

Again, this is the fundamental worldview of who we are and how we got here.

The fact that Jesus said "if you're not with me, you're against me" further behooves us to take notice.

Why should we love God? Because He loves us. He loves us because we are His children, and He created us in His own image.

...

Let's do a quick review what we've covered up until now:

- God exists (see Chapter 9 — Review: Existence of God).

- Man is of great value to God, like our children are to us.
- God must be authentic, much more authentic than us.
- If God is authentic, we can trust Him.
- He has a plan. He wants to live with us.
- He restricts Himself to make it happen.
- He sent Jesus to come down to give us the plan and to make it happen.
- He honors our free will to choose or reject Him.
- We are to believe in Him using our intellect.
- We should seek him.
- We are to obey Him and love each other.
- Trust the Plan.

PART 3
CREATION AND CHRISTIANITY

CHAPTER 16

THE CHRISTIAN VIEW OF CREATION

Hopefully by now, we have established that there is a God, and a loving God indeed who sent His only Son Jesus to redeem us, and that Jesus Himself provides one of the proofs of God's existence. Agreed? So, what's next?

Let's start at the beginning from a Christian view of creation. We believe that God created the world. The Old Testament account, shared with the Jews and Muslims, quotes God as identifying Himself as "I Am Who Am"—in other words He is existence itself.

According to the Bible (Genesis) and what we know from science, God, the Eternal *I Am* created the universe in the following order:

- Angels
- Satan, devils, and demons (after one-third of the angels rebelled)
- The Universe, perhaps through the Big Bang. "Let There Be Light."
- Planets

- Earth
- Animals
- Man (followed by Man corrupted)

Outside of "angels" and "man corrupted," this is consistent with science as we know it today. It all comes from a Divine Creator. It didn't "just happen."

LIFE IS A GIFT

We can see from all this that everything we have is a gift from God, wholly unearned and gratuitous in nature. We tend to pride ourselves on the gifts we have been given. If we are pretty, smart, or even naturally hardworking, these are gifts we have no control over. And of course, the ultimate gift we have received is the promise of salvation, gained by the supreme sacrifice of Jesus on the cross.

I'm good at accepting gifts. I put it in my pocket and say thanks. Then I ask for something else! That's how we are with God.

We should always be humble about our own gifts and tolerant of others. Many of our good qualities are gifts from God. I know in my case that the virtues that I have I come by naturally but the virtues that don't come naturally I don't have. I think this is true for most people. Our better qualities come from God as gifts; we must work to fill in the virtue gaps.

We must pity a man who, for all his remarkable gifts, refuses to recognize God as the principle of all the talents others see in him.

We must realize that logically, everything we have is a gift from God. Even things that we look upon as bad came from God to help us in some way that perhaps we can't see, like disciplining our children once again.

If we go through our lives with an understanding of life as a gift, it automatically generates a sense of gratitude in us.

Also, one thing I'm sure is true: to whom more is given, more is expected. This just makes sense.

WHAT IS OUR ULTIMATE GOAL?

Our goal is union and completion with God. The logical question is, did God provide us with a path? The answer is yes!

Here is what Christians believe:

- There is a God (see above) who is in charge of creation.

- God created man in His image and likeness.

- God gave us free will and respected our choices ... but we rejected Him (through sin).

- To give us hope of redemption God made His only begotten Son incarnate to suffer and die for our sins. Redemption means spending eternity with God and His people.

- Christianity is not a moral system of do's and don'ts; it is a relationship with God in Christ. Through prayer, faith will lead to an interior conversion and a deeper relationship with Jesus.

- God gives us the opportunity to believe this during our lives. Although God is hidden, He has revealed himself to us in certain ways:

HOW GOD REVEALS HIMSELF

Through Nature: Most people realize that the Creator of all this must be awesome when contemplating nature (e.g. sunsets, oceans, and mountains). An important distinction—nature is God's Creation, not God Himself!

Through Scripture: He revealed himself to the Jews by disclosing His name to them "I Am Who I Am." Also revealed himself as Father.

Through Prophets: People whom God chose to tell His story.

Through Covenants: God made covenants with Adam, Noah, Abraham, Moses, David, and Jesus. (Man broke each one.)

And finally, through taking the form of man, *Jesus Christ*.

ATTRIBUTES OF GOD (GOD IS . . .)

- Sovereign—God is in control of everything.
- Transcendent—God transcends Creation.
- God is the Creator of all things.
- God is immutable, meaning He never changes. Pure spirit is unchangeable and immutable.
- God is Mystery personified.
- God is All-Knowing.
- God is All Loving—God is Love.
- God is All Just. This is one reason why there is a heaven and a hell.
- God is All Merciful. If there is a way to cut us slack, God will find it.
- Only God exists entirely outside of time.

- God makes all things right. But in God's time not ours.
- God is always in action and always at rest.

God has revealed Himself as Father. Thus, our relationship to God is one of parent and child. This helps us understand how much God loves us and yet respects our decisions, even to turn away from Him.

> *For God, a thousand years is like a day and a day is like a thousand years.*
> 2 PETER 3:8

> *"...nor are your ways My ways—says the LORD. For as the heavens are higher than the earth, so are My ways higher than your ways, My thoughts higher than your thoughts."*
> ISAIAH 55:8

GOD IS TRINITY

Years ago, I was playing golf with a good friend of mine, and we got to talking about God. He said, "Well, you know God is not a person." I told him you may not think that God is a person but Jesus sure was, and Jesus claimed to be God and He *was* God.

There are many religions that don't really believe in the personhood of God. The Hindus and the Buddhists believe God is in us in some way, that we are God and the Earth is God, but Christianity is the only one that really comes out and says God is a person.

But doesn't it make sense that if the Creator is creating persons, that He's a person himself? For He must be able to relate to His creations.

God in the Bible stresses that we are made in the image and likeness of God, and if we are persons, it means that God is a person too. It can seem incredible to us that Creator of everything could be a person, but how could He not be?

What is a person? Persons are simply an *I,* a center of consciousness. Humans are a subset of persons, i.e., God is a non-human person. Persons generally have self-awareness, free will, high intellect, and are capable of love. God, being God, must have perfect (or super, as we say) levels of these, and contemplating this perfect level of self-awareness perhaps leads to a better understanding of the idea of Trinity. This is one of the hardest concepts for us to get our minds around, and for the purposes of this book, we don't need to. But I think we are all familiar with the concept of a Father, Son, and a Holy Spirit. I believe The Holy Spirit relates to God's self-awareness and His number one attribute—love.

Jesus opened a window in man's conception of who God is by revealing the idea that the Trinity, composed of God the Father, Jesus the Son, and the Holy Spirit, is unique in history to the Judeo-Christian faith. Jesus Himself is the one who taught this, referring to the Father and the Holy Spirit and Himself as God.

This concept is complex to understand, but is part of the New Covenant between God and Man. Through Jesus, we gain insights and understanding of our Creator.

If Jesus was God, this makes perfect sense. If He wasn't God, that means He was a liar and magician who seemed to know a lot about God and then died for our sins and rose from the dead.

ATTRIBUTES OF ANGELS: GOD'S FIRST CREATION

Angels are very cool and unique creatures. They are above us in the hierarchy of creation, like how high we are above the animals.

Angels are not disembodied people. They are a separate class of creatures. They are pure spirits and have a higher nature than man. Angels are not male and female but could be masculine or feminine.

God gave the angels a command (we do not know what), and some obeyed, some did not.

Women see angels more than men, probably because they are intuitive versus analytical and are thus more like angels. They are more on the same wavelength.

It is possible that the gods of ancient cultures were really angels.

Angels love God's creation of matter, but devils hate it. Angels love by an act of the will (goodwill) but they do not have emotions.

Angelology is a science based on two sources: 1) the Bible and 2) thousands of years of human experience.

Angels are aware of us, and we can communicate with them. They often come disguised and can appear to take physical form.

We are on a protected part of a great battlefield between angels and devils, extending to eternity. Angels work especially at moments of crisis for bodies, souls, and for nations.

We all have our very own guardian angel, according to Jesus:

> *See that you do not despise one of these little ones. For I tell you that their angels in heaven always see the face of my Father in heaven.*
>
> **MATTHEW 18:10**

We can't imagine pure spirits, but we can know them or understand their message.

Angels all have different personalities. They are all a different species like cats and dogs. They are arranged in a vertical hierarchy. We know this from Scripture, tradition, and teaching authority. Since angels are pure spirits, no two can be identical and equal—like a dog and cat and tree.

Angels have insights and are intuitive intelligences. They contemplate what they know: God, themselves, each other, us. They are never bored. Neither will we be in heaven.

In the scheme of creation, angels seem to fit in an upward ladder of existence:

- Minerals
- Animals
- Man
- Angels
- God

It fills a logical gap.

To be a Christian includes believing in angels because Jesus was in error if they do not exist. He talked about them all the time.

WHO IS SATAN/THE DEVIL?

Satan was an angel who wanted to be like God. *To have the knowledge of good and evil.* To be able to discern right from wrong on his own. Adam and Eve were the same way. Mankind is the same way. *It's all the same sin!* We want to be God and say, "I think this is right," and "I don't believe this," and "I think that."

Jesus came down to tell us to just obey. His message was one of love, obedience, and humility. But to accomplish this, you must have faith as well.

ATTRIBUTES OF DEMONS

Demons are pure spirits. They rebelled against God because they wanted to be God, to have the knowledge of Good and Evil, and to decide what is right. They inspire fear. They pervert God's revelations.

Satan hates the human race because we are made in the image and likeness of God. He was one of the most brilliant and highest created beings. His name, "Lucifer" means *to bear light*.

Lucifer knew he was splendid. He said, "I will not serve." He basically said, as Milton put it, "I would rather reign in hell than be a subject in heaven." He didn't like the notion of polluting spirit with matter and didn't go along with the program of creation.

Demons can (rarely) move matter supernaturally. They can possess us if we choose to invite them in. But they can't read our minds. And they don't know the future.

They tempt us through imagination or feeling.

The first temptation is to get us to doubt.

The second temptation is convince us to value what we think more than what God has said.

The essence of idolatry is putting something else in God's place. The essence of evil is believing *I am like God*. It's saying, "I will not serve, but you will serve me."

Satan is motivated by power over God. He knows God has his hands tied because of the rules He set up. He can't intervene too much. If He breaks the laws of creation, we lose our free will and become puppets and robots. To freely choose God, He must give us free will, even to reject Him.

Enemy-occupied territory—that is what this world is.

C.S. Lewis

The sight of the devil is one of the principal torments of hell. The *Miserific vision* is the opposite of the *Beatific vision* of God in heaven.

Oddly, more women are affected by demons than men, perhaps because they can, in turn, drag men down, or maybe it's an extension of the original temptation with Eve. Youth are also affected more than the elderly.

There are three levels of demonic influence on men and women:

1. **Temptation:** we all have this.
2. **Oppression:** fairly rare, but it happens.
3. **Possession:** exceedingly rare.

Jesus said the reason for His coming was to defeat Satan.

According to Christianity, evil entered our world because of Satan's fall, so it has a personal character. Jesus Christ spoke directly with Satan at the moment of His temptation (Matthew 4:1-11). He cast out demons (Mark 1:21-28), and the apostles did also (Acts 5:16), so they were not addressing illusions. The Apostle Peter warned his fellow Christians that Satan is a real and dangerous presence:

> *Be self-controlled and alert. Your enemy the devil, prowls around like a roaring lion looking for someone to devour.*
>
> **1 Peter 5-8**

Likewise, St. Paul emphasizes that *Satan himself is masquerading as an angel of light* to deceive humans (2 Corinthians 11:14). These passages and many more instruct on the reality of evil.

ATTRIBUTES OF ANIMALS

- Bodies without souls.
- They lack self-reflection.
- They have no knowledge of immaterial objects.
- Animals have a strong instinct for survival and continuation of the species. They are focused on eating and procreating.
- Still, animals are protected by God, do His will, and have an intelligence that we don't fully understand.

ATTRIBUTES OF MAN

Man was created in the image and likeness of God:

- Finite body, infinite soul. (Hybrid of physical body and spiritual soul.)
- Have either masculine or feminine souls.
- Exists in time.
- Spirit side is angel-like.
- Endowed with free will. (God gives us the freedom to rebel.)

Our material brain is much less powerful than our souls' spiritual intelligence, so we seldom see things as fully as possible at once. But an angel has no such limit and hence sees everything as fully as possible at once. So he cannot go back on his decision and say: "I see it differently now; I wish I had not done that."

In his original state, man communicated openly with God and was protected from the elements by God. However, through temptation by the devil, he committed the same sin as the devil—aspiring to be God and to have the knowledge of good and evil. Instead of obedience, gratitude, and love, man used his free will to turn away from his Creator. "I'll call you if I need you." I know better. It's saying to the Lord, "I don't really trust you."

PRIMEVAL STORY OF REBELLION

Adam and Eve were afraid if they acknowledged God, they would have to conform to His will. We are the same today. Adam and Eve opened the door to evil.

We need salvation from sin and evil. We are part matter so we can change (repent). We are equipped to resist temptation.

The mystery of the creation of the physical world is fulfilled only in the creation of man. Only through man is the material world united with God the Creator. Man is rational because he was created in the image and likeness of God. The material world is entirely passive and depends on God totally.

This makes total sense. Why would God create the universe if there was no end game, no authentic reason? Man is the reason, and as we have seen science is beginning to reveal this.

WHAT ABOUT GHOSTS?

Ghosts are spirits, or souls of dead human beings which are still operating on an Earth-bound plane. Ghosts are ghosts because:

- They don't realize they are dead yet.
- They were so attached to material places or possessions that they couldn't detach themselves from them and leave.

- They are working out some purification, penance, or purgatory.
- They are consoling bereaved loved ones.

There is enormous evidence of ghosts in all cultures. There are three types of ghosts, according to Peter Kreeft in his book *Everything You Ever Wanted to Know About Heaven: But Never Dreamed of Asking*:

1. They seem to be working out unfinished earthly business or suffering purgatorial purification until they are released from their earthly business. These ghosts are the ones who barely made it to purgatory, who feel little or no joy yet and need to learn many painful lessons about their lives on Earth.

2. Second, there are malicious and deceptive spirits—and since they are deceptive, they hardly ever appear malicious. These are probably the ones who respond to conjuring séances. They probably come from hell. Even the chance of that happening should be sufficient to turn us away from temptations to necromancy (communication with spirits).

3. Third, there are bright, happy spirits of dead friends and family—especially spouses—who appear unbidden at God's will, not ours, with messages of hope and love. They seem to come from heaven.

The thing to realize is all this goes on with God's knowledge. There is nothing hidden from the Lord.

THE TEN COMMANDMENTS: GOD'S CODE FOR US TO LIVE BY

Better known in Western culture as the Ten Suggestions, most people cannot even name the commandments that were given to Moses 4,000 years ago and reemphasized by Jesus 2,000 years ago. (Many can only name numbers 5, 7, and 8.)

1. I am the Lord your God. You shall worship the Lord your God and Him only shall you serve.
2. You shall not take the name of the Lord your God in vain.
3. Remember to keep holy the Sabbath day.
4. Honor your father and your mother.
5. You shall not kill.
6. You shall not commit adultery.
7. You shall not steal.
8. You shall not bear false witness against your neighbor.
9. You shall not covet your neighbor's wife.
10. You shall not covet your neighbor's goods.

I think the First Commandment is perhaps the most ignored of all the commandments. We all have "masters" that occupy our attention, actions, and thoughts. What a world this would be if everybody followed these ten simple commandments, which we have had for 4,000 years!

SIN

No matter how bad Satan can be, man cannot be affected by him if he persists in obedience to God. By submitting himself to Satan's temptation and misusing the freedom of choice granted by the Creator, man became the perpetuator of evil in our world through sin. Satan is not the only one guilty of the evil in our world, and we are not just victims lacking any responsibility. **God has put a limit to Satan's power** against us humans so that he can never overwhelm us (1 Corinthians 10:13). Therefore, we have absolute freedom to refuse evil. Always remember, no matter how insidious Satan is, God is bigger, much bigger!

The Three Root Sins: everybody has one of these as a primary tendency:

- **Pride**: the tendency to equalize my judgment to God's. (Anger and impatience are signs of pride.)
- **Sensuality**: comfort is the principle of action.
- **Vanity**: to be a source of admiration

To discern this, look at the motives for everything you do.

These are the "raw materials" from which vices spring. They are the deep-seated tendencies toward selfishness that we originally inherited at birth, and we call this concupiscence.

DEATH

Most people have this huge thing lurking in the background of their psyche, too terrible to even think about — death. We don't even want to talk or think about it ... *when it's 100% our future!* You'd think it would be all we thought about, but it's not. Why? Because our faith in what we cannot see is weak, and we are concerned with what is happening now, even though we could die at any moment.

The reason we don't want to think about it is that deep down, we know that everything we're doing on Earth, everything we accomplish, even our family and our friends, all turn to ashes when we die. It's our biggest problem and depressing to think about, so we don't!

In Genesis, the reason we die is explained simply. We sinned, and therefore, separated ourselves from God. Sin is the separation from God, of which physical disintegration is only the outward sign.

But death was actually an act of kindness from God, who did not want us to live forever physically in a condition of separation from Him, a living death (or hell on Earth).

> *Behold the man has become like one of us, knowing good and evil; and now lest he take also of the tree of life and eat, and live forever.*
>
> **Genesis 3:22-24**

We are lost through sin to God. This just means that God owns us in the first place. However, the image of God in man, though disfigured, was never really lost. God provided the antidote.

When Jesus famously raised Lazarus after being dead for four days, Jesus said to Martha, "I am the resurrection and the life. Whoever believes in Me will live, even though he dies. And everyone who lives and believes in Me will never die. Do you believe this?"

Jesus is telling us that He is the answer to our biggest problem, and as usual, He backed it up by raising Lazarus from the dead.

Faith takes the sting out of the thought of death. By instinct, nobody wants to die, but if you believe a Kingdom is waiting for you, it takes a lot of the fear out that we usually have.

Logically, death should be something we look forward to if seen through the eyes of faith. Eternal bliss united with our loving Creator. Beats what we have down here, no?

HEAVEN

About ten years ago, *U.S. News and World Report* surveyed its readership, asking readers if they thought certain famous people would go to heaven or hell. For instance, the results showed that 52% thought Bill Clinton would go to heaven. Eight percent thought Hitler would go to heaven. Mother Teresa was 80%. Then, they asked them if they thought they would go to heaven themselves. This generated the highest percentage—88%. So, most people, while having a dim view of others' chances, think they are more likely to go to heaven than Mother Teresa!

This means to me that we all need a wake-up call.

Our life is very short, and eternity is very long. We need to get this right, boys!

Life is a great deal. We have many gifts from God in this world, but the ultimate is in the afterlife with Him in heaven. Religion puts this all into perspective, realizing and reminding us that the next world is far more critical than this one and infinitely longer.

Knowing and understanding that this life is a precursor to the real life gives us a sense of calm and peace because we know that the hardships we are facing now are temporary. The next life (which we don't understand now) is better than anything we could conceive of down here on Earth. We know this from scriptural references and from the great saints of the last 2,000 years who have had visions of heaven far beyond our comprehension.

It's hard to picture what heaven is like. Sometimes we think, "what do we do all day up there? Just learn to play the harp?" I believe this is another case where we just have to trust God.

> **We either must trust God that heaven is wonderful or trust the devil that hell is not so bad!**

We do not know exactly what heaven will be like. It is beyond the realm of human experience. Yet God's revelation through Scripture provides some clues. We know for sure that in heaven, we will be in the presence of God. We will "see him as he is, face to face" (see 1 John 3:2). We will experience God's ultimate self-communication to us—what has been called the "Beatific Vision," a union so profound that it will be less like gazing upon God and more like being joined to Him.

St. Paul had a vision of heaven and said, "eyes have not seen nor ears heard" what God has prepared for us. St. Thomas Aquinas also had a vision of heaven. He described the Beatific Vision as: "The most perfect union with God is the most perfect human happiness and the goal of the whole of the human life, a gift that must be given to us by God."

While we cannot yet grasp what this will be like, we must trust that this unending experience of God will be beyond anything we can imagine. It is easy to think that if and when we enter into eternal life, we will bring with us our memories, emotions, and desires, but these will be transformed as our very selves will be renewed in the presence of God. What had been important to us while on Earth will no longer be significant.

The Kingdom is Heaven. We have an unbelievably benevolent King who wants to share his fortune and life with us. Faith is a gift from God to which we yield.

We are there in the first place because we yield our obedience. In this circumstance, we could never have thought of disagreement.

Keep in mind there are some things we just don't know. We only know the basics, but God has given us the essential things that we need. There are still many mysteries, but God is giving us a road map of how to live our lives and what to expect in the next life.

So, we should focus on this and align our will with God's will. This trusting of the Lord brings peace and happiness on Earth, and that is what we are all striving for anyway.

HELL: YOU DON'T WANT TO GO THERE

I talked a bit about heaven, but I haven't mentioned hell often. Most people would rather not think about it, and the culture wants to make us believe it doesn't exist.

But wait a second, why were we headed to hell in the first place? Why did we need saving? Because when we had a free choice, we sided with the devil and his lies in the Garden of Eden narrative. Now, one might say wait, that wasn't me. That was Adam and Eve or my ancestors. Yes, it was you because, as shown in these pages, in addition to that Original Sin, we continually commit the same sins they did.

The fact that hell exists is why Saint Paul said:

We are to work out our salvation in fear and trembling.

But here's the bottom line about heaven and hell. Heaven is a whole lot better than we think it is, and hell is a whole lot worse. Why do I say that? In the Catholic faith, there are people that we call mystics. Mystics pray virtually all the time and are immersed in contemplative prayer. These people go deeper and get an understanding that the rest of us don't. There's a book I recommend called *The End of the Present World and the Mysteries of the Future Life* by Father

Charles Arminjon, which brilliantly describes the afterlife, based on Scripture and personal insights.

John Paul II wrote that hell is the eternal fixation on nothingness. The forever knowledge that you blew it.

Heaven cannot be where everyone is forgiven but still ducks God. We will be transformed, but we must be willing to be changed.

> *There are only two kinds of people in the end: those who say to God "Thy will be done" and those to whom God says, in the end, 'Thy will be done'. All that are in Hell, choose it. Without that self-choice, there could be no Hell. No soul that seriously and constantly desires joy will ever miss it. Those who seek find. To those that knock it is opened.*
>
> C.S. Lewis

PURGATORY: ANOTHER GIFT FROM GOD

The idea of purgatory is that there exists a state of being of our soul after we die and before we go to heaven. It is a time of purging our souls and suffering temporarily.

Most religions don't believe in purgatory, so if it does exist, nobody prays for the souls' residing there. Think about that.

I am a Catholic, and we believe there is a purgatory between heaven and hell and that there are biblical references and strong theological reasons behind this belief. I'm not going to go into it now, but let's say the Catholics are right for a second. It's important to note that 100% of the people who go to purgatory will one day end up in heaven. Even though people are suffering while working out unresolved earthly issues, it is a happy place because everyone knows they are saved.

I am a numbers guy, so here's how I look at it:

Jesus told Peter that the gates of hell shall not withstand against the Church He was creating. So that means to me that more than 50% of people will go to heaven. I believe it will be much more than that, as good will prevail, and God will have a sweeping victory. But some, from private revelation by the Blessed Virgin Mary, believe that most souls destined for heaven go to purgatory first, and it is essential that we pray for them to lessen the extent of their suffering there. They are not ready. Purgatory is a gift from God in the sense that these people, who perhaps constitute a majority of souls, are not prepared for heaven but are given an intermediate place to make that possible. Otherwise, many more people would end up in hell if it were not for purgatory.

I have read estimates that more than 100 billion people have lived since the beginning of time. But only the Catholics even believe in purgatory. Few non-Christian faiths believe in purgatory, nor do the non-Catholic Christians. Of current living people, this is only about 15%, and of those, only about a third are really practicing their faith. So, only 5% of the people on Earth pray for our loved ones in purgatory.

Remember that purgatory was a basic tenant of belief in the Christian church for more than 1,500 years. Jews, Catholics, and the Eastern Orthodox have always historically proclaimed the reality of the final purification. It was not until the Protestant Reformation in the sixteenth century that anyone denied this doctrine.

CHAPTER 17

THE BIBLE: GOD TALKS TO US

How do we know God? What do we know about the word of God? Does it not make sense that if God created the world, He would wish to communicate with us? Uh, yes!

How do we know what God wants? The Bible is the **living word of God** and is all about Man's search for God and God's search for Man. God wants us to seek Him. The Bible says, "Ask and you shall receive, seek and you shall find, knock and the door shall be opened to you."

I don't know about you, but I find this a fantastic statement if it is indeed from God himself. It is because who else could say that? You mean all I have to do is ask? But unless we are believers, we don't ask.

From my personal experience, this is a deal that God honors. You don't always get exactly what you asked for but often it's even better. It's very much like the parent-child relationship, which is a great analogy. Often our kids ask for things that wouldn't be good for them, and we end up giving them something much better. That's what's going on here.

One of the most fundamental things that God desires is for us to seek Him. To strive to believe. If you are a beginner, you can even qualify it first and say, "Lord, if you are up there, show me the way." He will answer, believe me.

I believe the best ways to seek God are prayer and reading the Bible, which is still the most purchased and read book and in every hotel room. The Bible is an excellent collection of truth and is widely believed to be divinely inspired. It doesn't mean that the Bible doesn't require interpretation and should be taken literally in every sense. That's why we have Bible study. But our agnostic culture now looks down on the Bible "stories" with condescension when, in fact, it contains the great truth of the ages.

Skeptics might say, "Wait—we don't even know who wrote the Bible." That's not true. The Bible is a library and collection of books, and we have a good idea of who wrote what. But the way I look at it, the thing that gives the Bible the most credibility is Jesus Christ Himself. He is immensely credible and authentic, and the Bible is all about the coming of Jesus and His life on Earth. He constantly validated Scripture by referring to it and fulfilling its prophecies. The New Testament chronicles His life and mighty deeds.

If the Bible is not the word of God, then what is it, and where did it come from? In a sense, that would make it even more impressive. It is not hard to believe that if there is a God, He could direct us to write something like that. But if there is not a God, well then it's like the universe—random and disordered—just wrote it by itself. The wisdom and elegance of Scripture hold the secrets of life, code to live by, prophets whose words came true, redemption and promise of salvation ... from the beginning of the world, to the revelation of God in the world, to agreements God made with man; to the Ten Commandments on how we should live our lives ... and then to Jesus Christ; salvation history and the promise of everlasting life — it's all there.

In his book *12 Rules for Life: An Antidote to Chaos,* author Jordan Peterson says biblical stories are acted out every day across humanity. Most popular stories mimic the biblical stories, and it's in our souls to recognize these stories. We have an instinct for religion.

Recently, I was reading the amazing Bible passage of the Transfiguration. If you don't know the story, Jesus goes up the mountain with three of his disciples and not only do Moses and Elijah appear, but Jesus's clothes become dazzling white, and God the Father speaks audibly to them all! Many religions believe that when we die, we become one with nature or the universe, and we are spread among the cosmos, implying that we lose our identity in some way. It strikes me that the Transfiguration is God's way of showing us that we do not lose our individuality in the afterlife. Peter, James, and John go up the mountain with Jesus ... and then Moses and Elijah are there, about a thousand years after their deaths. There is discussion among them. Peter wanted to make them tents! I mean, this is so cool.

Consider Pentecost, where the Holy Spirit descends upon the disciples. They went forth and spoke in tongues, and people of 20 different languages understood simultaneously. When has that ever happened? How could they even make that up?

Scripture helps us to *know the truth*, in Luke's words, because it offers, through inspired experiences and authors, a trustworthy story of what we need to know about God and how God has entered human life. It is the written testimony to a series of interventions in which God reveals himself in human history.

SALVATION

The Bible is the story of our salvation. We can see clearly from the Bible that God looks less at the totality of our lives than our disposition at the end of it. There are many examples in Scripture where people are wicked, repent, and are saved.

And the opposite is true. Some Protestant denominations insist that if we profess that *Jesus is our Lord and Savior* at any moment, we are then irrevocably saved. We are saved, but it's not irrevocable. We can blow it because we have free will, which allows us to turn against God. That's why the devil is always after us and never gives up. Do people who profess Jesus as their Lord and Savior never have temptations afterward? I think they do. The devil knows he can still derail them.

THE EXTRAORDINARY ACCURACY OF BIBLICAL PROPHESIES

Peter Pilt of the *My Thoughts* blog wrote a compelling compilation of biblical prophetic accuracy. Here are some excerpts:

> *He stretches out the north over empty space;*
> *He hangs the Earth on nothing. (Job 26)*

That was a radical thought until just a few hundred years ago. How did Job know that, perhaps 8,000 years ago? All Scripture is given by inspiration! Nobody believed the Earth was round until 1492. "Columbus, you're going to sail off the end of the Earth," ... but 700 years before Christ, Isaiah said that God "sits upon the circle of the Earth." Circle in Hebrew means globe or sphere. *(Isaiah 40:22)*

Number of Stars

In 150 BC, an astronomer named Hipparchus laid down his pencil and smiled, "It's done!" He believed he had counted all the stars in the sky—1,022! That was the number used in universities for 250 years. Then Ptolemy came along and said: "1,022—that's ridiculous. There's 1,026!" He found four more! And that was science for 1,300 years. Then Galileo came along with his invention, the first crude telescope; he looked through it for the first time and gasped. We know now that there are billions and billions of stars in each of the galaxies, which are innumerable!

What did the Bible say long before any of them were even born?

As the host of heaven cannot be numbered. (Jeremiah 33)

Prophetic Accuracy

No book in history has dared to predict the future to the degree the Bible has without being proven wrong.

For the sake of time, let's narrow it down to just the prophecies that dealt with the coming of Christ 2,000 years ago.

More than 300 direct prophecies in question, like:

Isaiah 7:14—He would be born of a virgin.
Luke 1:7—it happened!

Micah 5:2—was born in Bethlehem.
Luke 2:4—that happened!

Genesis 49:10—born of tribe of Judah.
Matthew 3:3—that happened!

Psalm 78:2—speaks in parables.
Matthew 13:34—that happened!

Zechariah 9:9—ride on the colt of a donkey.
Matthew 21—that happened!

Isaiah 61—healed broken-hearted.
Luke 4:18—that happened!

Isaiah 53:3—rejected by own.
John 1:11—that happened!

Isaiah 53:7—stand silent before accusers.
Mark 15:5—that happened!

Psalm 22:18—cast lots for His robe.
John 19:23—that happened!

Psalm 22—(hundreds of years before crucifixion was invented or thought of), prophets said they would pierce His hands and feet—and it happened!

Psalm 22:1—"my God, why have you forsaken me?"
Matthew 27:46—that happened!

Zechariah 11:2—sold by enemies for 30 pieces of silver.
Matthew 26:15—that happened!

Isaiah 53:9—buried with the rich.
Matthew 27—that happened!

One skeptic said, "certainly, this is the most striking coincidence of details."

Dr. Charles Ryrie points out that, by the law of chance, it would require 2 hundred billion Earths—each populated with four billion people—to come up with one person who could achieve one hundred accurate prophecies without any errors in sequence. But, in Christ's coming alone, there were not one hundred, but "more than 300 prophecies fulfilled! And that's just the tip of the iceberg—the prophecies dealing with His first coming!

CHAPTER 18

PRAYER: WE TALK TO GOD

Prayer is not just words but a sense of gratitude. Prayer is a gift. Based in humility. It pleases God. Raising of our hearts and minds to God. It allows us to connect to our Creator.

Prayer is to encounter God's thirst for us. We respond to God's love with love.

Prayer is a habit of being in communion with God.

Most of us are familiar with the Our Father prayer. This prayer fascinates me because it gives us insight into God's mind. It is an excellent prayer because we know **God Himself asked us to pray this way** when Jesus was asked, "How should we pray?" If you take the first sentence of the prayer, Jesus is establishing God as a Father to us and His name "Be Hallowed," i.e., exalted. This recalls the Second Commandment: Thou Shalt Not Take the Name of the Lord Thy God in Vain. This is really important to God. And we can imagine this ourselves. How would we like it if every time our kids did something wrong, they would curse us? God commands respect just as any father would.

The name of Jesus is powerful. Jesus offers Himself, His spirit, and His Holy Name. His name protects our souls. That's why we must never violate the Second Commandment and take Jesus's or God's name in vain. If we are aware of this, it is pretty easy to stop. But people need to be made aware of the Ten Commandments.

The Our Father then says, *Thy Kingdom come, Thy will be done*, which tells us to look to heaven . . . and trust His will. It is great hope and simplicity combined. Then He says, *Give us this day, our daily bread*, which again says ask Me for what you need, and it shows that He wants to be involved in a conversation with us. The ending of the prayer talks of forgiveness and makes it clear that this is conditional. He will forgive us IF we forgive others. So, dear reader, it's a two-way street, but the good news is, He is saying our sins and the things we have done wrong in our lives are not the problem. Forgiveness is the issue; we are getting it from Him, but we need to do the same thing to others. Forgiveness is not an option.

Again, this is pretty simple, although I'm not saying it's easy.

So, in our daily lives, we encounter people who don't behave the way they should or the way we would like them to behave. God is telling us to cut them some slack because Jesus's sacrifice on the cross is the ultimate slack-cutting. We're supposed to mimic that as best we can.

It's also interesting that the last two parts of the Our Father prayer involve the devil. When the prayer says, *lead us not into temptation*, it is saying, don't let the devil tempt us, and when it says *deliver us from evil*, it's saying keep the devil away from us. It also shows what a problem Satan is. Again, these are God's words delivered by Jesus, and you can be assured of this (unless, of course, you believe Jesus was a con man and a liar!).

If your dad buys you a car when you're 16 and tells you to be home by 11:00 on Friday nights and not to have certain people in the car with you, and you break all the rules — there will be consequences from your dad. Also, if you break the rules, it's worse if you don't call him.

That's what prayer is like. We all sit down here and break God's relatively simple laws, but if we don't communicate with our Father, we're not "calling" Him either. We're shutting ourselves off. God is our Father like our dads were, and we strongly desire our children to communicate with us. Prayer is just talking to God and telling him what's going on. He wants that. And if we don't pray, we are cutting ourselves off from our Maker.

God wants His will to be done on Earth and in heaven. Can you blame Him for that? He's the one who created everything, so shouldn't He be the final word on everything? Who are we to resist the will of God?

If we were God and we totally bailed out our rebellious and ungrateful kids, would we want them to know that we bailed them out and that they be reminded of it now and then? Of course, the answer is yes because that's human nature. But it's God's nature, too. He went the extra mile for us in a radical way. In our communication with Him, in prayer, He wants us to meditate upon the events of His passion, death, and resurrection. As Catholics, we call this the rosary, one of the most emblematic signs of the Catholic faith.

According to Catholic tradition, the Blessed Mother herself instituted the rosary. In the thirteenth century, she was said to have appeared to St. Dominic (founder of the Dominicans), given him a rosary, and asked that Christians pray the Hail Mary, Our Father, and Glory Be prayers instead of the Psalms.

So here we have the mother of Jesus appearing to a very holy person and saying, "The Psalms are wonderful, but I want your flock to remember what my son did!"

Makes sense to me!

CHAPTER 19

FREE WILL

Most of us believe that, as human beings, we have free will, and this is also one of the basic tenets of theology, especially Christianity. If we did not have free will, we would not be able to freely choose God or choose to do right or even wrong. There would be no concept of sin without free will. Again, we see that God is limiting himself by giving us free will, making Him subject to Man's judgment.

One of the most vexing issues for me personally is the understanding that although I know that we have free will, I also know that we are all very much programmed by two things: 1) our personality/genetics, which is God-given, and something we are born with and 2) our environment and the experiences that we have. These shape us profoundly to the point where one must ask where the free will comes in.

But understanding how much we and our fellow man are programmed by things we have no control over can help us better understand our brothers and sisters and allow us to cut them some slack as Jesus does us—for we don't know if, in any given situation, a person is acting from his genetic and environmental programming or his free will. We tend to treat people as if everything they do is of their free will, and we tend to treat ourselves as if everything we do is not our fault, and we couldn't help it!

Let's take an extreme example of a mafia hitman who was instructed to kill somebody. He has tremendous "environmental" pressure on him to do this job. His situation in life is not of his doing because he was born into it. He might have been an entirely different person in a different family. Also there may be genetic reasons. Maybe he's blessed with excellent hand-eye coordination and was selected to carry this out. If he was naturally a clutz he may have been chosen to keep the books.

However, his free will could have said no this is wrong and I'm not going to do this. His flawed nature from birth complicates his ability to use his free will and do the right thing regardless of consequences. In the end, society comes down on the side of free will and will hold him responsible.

Researchers have studied this phenomenon and concluded that what we have even more than free will is a "free won't."

Famous researcher Benjamin Libet did many experiments on the brain and decision-making, studying brain waves just before a decision was made. He determined that our capacity to make affirmative choices is measurable, but brainwaves can't measure the capacity to choose not to do something. He concluded that this process must come from outside the brain and body, from the soul. This is more of a "free won't!" This dovetails with the Ten Commandments, eight of which are things not to do — Thou shalt not... The other two — Thou Keep Holy the Lord's Day and Honor Thy Father and Mother could be looked at as *don't neglect God or your parents.*

A priest friend brought more clarity to this conundrum to me. He drew a chart (nearby) that outlined the forces that affect our behavior and how we react to problems and situations in our lives. Of course, we can't know the actual percentages but say roughly 40% of our "programming" is determined by our God-given genetics and the environment in which we are raised and live. Perhaps 30% is estimated to be from our flawed nature—our tendency towards sin—which we are born with. This is called Original Sin, and it is a significant issue for all of us. The final component is our true free will, which can overcome all the rest. We have the freedom to choose, but start from a significantly compromised position. This is the challenge of all people on this Earth and is why we need God and religion in our lives. It's tough to do this on our own.

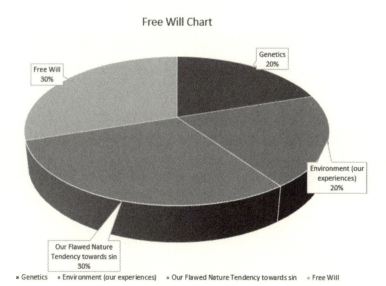

CHAPTER 20

THE SECRET TO LIFE

God really had to give us free will because if He didn't, we would just be puppets controlled by Him. The *secret to life* is that we take this free will and give it back to Him and say, "You are not the puppeteer because my free will is that Your will be done. I still have plenty of free will within this parameter, and I will try to align my will as best I can with Yours."

If we understand that and accept it, then everything in this life and the next falls into place immediately. We do have to work at it because we start from a position where we don't really know God's will.

Even Jesus—who we are taught was 100% man and 100% God—struggled with this. What did He do the night before He was tortured and killed? He asked God if He could get out of it somehow, showing His humanness by saying, "Not My will be done, but Thy will be done."

To understand and embrace this, we must ask, seek, and knock.

In this life, you must strive for what you want. But it would help if you wanted the right thing. If you aim for the wrong thing, you'll never be happy in this life and jeopardize the next life. The right thing is God's will.

Your life should be ordered just as the universe is ordered.

Start by saying this prayer. "Lord, if you're out there, help me believe in You." Then you can graduate to ... "Lord I believe, help my unbelief!"

GRATITUDE

If somebody does something good for you, the natural response is gratitude. This is all the truer if someone gives you incredible gifts and literally saves your life. Gratitude should be our attitude toward God and is part of the secret of life. God, our Creator, is not commanding this. He's asking us to recognize reality.

Does this mean we must submit to God? Uh ... yep!

Question: Are you okay with that? Because that's what we're talking about here. The definition of submission is *the action or fact of accepting or yielding to a superior force or the will or authority of another person.*

Now we're getting down to the nitty-gritty. Many people resist submitting to anyone. But we do in the course of our lives. We submit to our bosses and, in many ways, our spouses. God wants us to submit to Him freely, not as a slave driver but as a Father and friend. Another phrase that is used is *docility to the Holy Spirit.* It says I trust you, Lord, and I'm on board with whatever You have in store for me.

Consider the thought that God *wants* me here. The Creator of the universe is sustaining me personally. I would not be here if He did not actively want me to be on Earth.

If we *really* believed in God, it would fix many of the problems in the world and ease much of the suffering. It's the root of much of the strife in the world. Belief in God changes your worldview in a radical but very positive way. You don't worry so much about death.

Even sickness takes on meaning when seen as part of His Permissive Will. The temporary nature of hardship is brought into the light of an eternity without it.

Political movements based on Man as the center of the world rather than God try to establish a utopia on Earth through force and coercion rather than trust in God and the promise of salvation in a heavenly Kingdom.

If you don't believe in God or are weak in your faith, it's likely not your fault because this godless world has so influenced you. Please be aware that you are in the minority. Don't make the mistake of believing everyone else in history was stupid. They weren't!

In the past, the meaning of life was linked to the challenge of simple survival. Staying alive meant forming a family and having children to care for you in your old age. The knowledge that sudden death could happen at any moment required attention to spiritual issues. Doing those things provided deep satisfaction that went beyond survival.

Life in an age of plenty and security requires none of those things. For the great majority of people living in advanced societies, it is easily possible to go through life accompanied by social companions and serial sex partners, having a good time, and dying in old age with no reason to think one has done anything significant.

If you believe that's all there is, that the *purpose of life* is to while away the time as pleasantly as possible, you are wrong. There is a transcendent meaning to life, which you were created for, and you have a responsibility to God and yourself to investigate, pursue, and develop.

We should give thought to the fact that we will be judged. God is mercy and love, but He is also justice and truth, and there will be a day of reckoning. The reason we ignore Christ is because of affection for sin. We love the darkness more than the light. You do not drift to heaven along with everyone else rebelling. You must make a choice.

As Christians, we are constantly told that we cannot earn salvation. Jesus has done that for us. Indeed, this is true, but in another sense, we do have to earn it. We must make that choice. Jesus will come to *judge the living and the dead,* but what will He judge? He will consider everything, but we will be judged on our belief in God and how well we lived our life by loving God with our whole heart and soul and our neighbor as ourselves.

Jesus in the Agony in the Garden before His Passion said, "My heart is troubled even to death." The devil was showing Him the ingratitude of man for centuries. Angels came to comfort Him. But He saw too all the faithful of the future.

It's not enough to be part of the crowd that is just kind of following Jesus. We need to be a true friend of Jesus.

I forget who said the theme song in hell is "I Did It My Way." We tend to just want to do our own thing, where life is a cafeteria, and I pick what I want to do or believe in.

We must pity a man who, for all his remarkable gifts, refuses to recognize God as the principle of all the talents others see in him.

You have forgotten God who gave you birth.

Deuteronomy 32

CHAPTER 21

SUMMARY: OUR STAIRWAY TO HEAVEN

To summarize: Does God exist? Yes. We know this because everything could not have happened by itself, especially the laws of nature and our highly complex DNA software.

Faith must follow the recognition that there is a God, the Creator of the universe. Otherwise, we are rebels against our Creator. God must be a better god than we would be if we were God.

There are barriers to belief that make it difficult for many to embrace these truths. They do not believe a loving God would allow so much pain and suffering. Remember that life is short, and eternity is very long.

He is hidden, yes, but he showed Himself in Jesus.

Deep down, we are afraid of changing our life. This is where we need to shake off our genetics, environment, and selfish tendencies and step up our stairway to heaven!

We should remember that there have been thousands of astounding physical miracles in the name of Jesus Christ since He was on Earth. This should bring us great confidence in our faith.

Who was Jesus? He was a miracle worker who healed the sick, raised the dead to life, walked on water, turned water into wine, and most importantly, predicted his own torture and death and that he would rise again on the third day and then actually do it. Jesus had to be either a crazy person, a liar, or God. **Crazy people and liars do not do the things Jesus did. So logically, He was God incarnated as man.**

Why are we here? It is a test to see if we are with God or against Him, and He will respect our choice, which is made from the free will that He gave us. Eternal bliss in heaven or eternal damnation in hell hangs in the balance for all of us. All the things in life mean nothing compared to this one thing. **We cannot be in a state of rebellion against God. That is the test.**

The Bible is how God speaks to us. We have a gift called free will, and we have the opportunity to choose God who created us and to trust him to the point where we hand him the reins, and we say, "Not my will be done but Your will be done."

WHAT AM I SUPPOSED TO DO? A CALL TO ACTION

Maybe now you're saying, "Okay, Bob, you convinced me, or okay, I'm a little curious about this now. It sure looks like there must be a God, which makes it incumbent on me to believe that Jesus Christ is Lord. What should I do?" A great place to start is to buy a Bible and just read the word of God and let it speak to you. I would recommend reading the New Testament first. Listen to the words of Jesus and see if you agree they have the "ring of truth."

When the disciples asked Jesus, "What are we supposed to do?" he said "Go ye and teach all nations." It's likely you're not quite ready for that now but you never know — with God all things are possible!

I'm a Roman Catholic, and so when you think you're ready, my recommendation is to join the Catholic Church. The way to do that is to find a local parish. There are approximately 17,000 parishes in the United States. They have an OCIA program in each one to educate you about the Catholic faith.

In writing this section my goal is not to sound too Catholic. Forgive me if I do. That's not the purpose of this book. The purpose of this book is to ask you, dear reader, to please not be a "none" (religiously unaffiliated). Being a none makes no sense. It's illogical!

It could be that you have some past affiliation with one of the Christian non-Catholic denominations and are more comfortable there. There are more than 35,000 Evangelical or Protestant denominations, and there is one near you. Although I recommend the Catholic Church, I also recommend baby steps as you go along with this journey. Sometimes you have to date before you get married.

The Catholic Church was initially instituted by Christ when he said, "Thou art Peter, and upon this Rock I will build my Church." He then *gave Peter the keys to heaven,* which seems to me of great importance and significance when considering this. The Catholic Church is a 2,000-year-old intellectual philosophy rich in tradition, deep in biblical context, with an extraordinary intimacy with Christ through His sacraments. This richness includes the Mass, Eucharist, great saints, martyrs, feast days, miracles, rituals, relics, great devotion (not worship) to the Blessed Mother, rosary, apparitions of Mary, guardian angels, and the Magesterium, the central teaching authority of the Church. This in turn generates the Catechism which is a comprehensive guide of 2,000 years of scriptural and philosophical Christian thought. The Catholics also built magnificent architecture—churches with masterpieces and sculptures all designed to bring great glory to

God. The Catholic Church is also the largest charitable organization on the planet, created the college system, the scientific method and its monks preserved the manuscripts of the Bible in the Middle Ages.

The Protestants threw most of this out in the sixteenth century during the Reformation, believing that instead of bringing people closer to Jesus, this was obscuring the real truth of the Christian faith. Protestantism emphasizes a simple one-on-one personal relationship with Jesus Christ, underpinned by deep biblical devotion. This is the whole goal of Christianity anyway and the Protestants believe the direct approach is best. This is a different perspective than the Catholics and it seems to me it suits a lot of people. It allows another major path to Jesus with each having more than a billion members.

The Protestant Reformation happened in the early sixteenth century. They agreed that the Church needed to be reformed (which it did) and agreed with the basic tenets of the faith but they could not agree on lesser doctrinal issues, and that's why it has splintered into many smaller denominations. I believe that the split of the Christian churches was a bad thing, and it was followed by a 100-year war. However, *God makes all things right* and we see that the non-Catholic Christians have converted millions of people to the faith. Great preachers like Billy Graham, David Honggi Cho, Pat Robertson, Oral Roberts, and John Wesley have borne much fruit.

The analogy I use is that the Catholic Church is the Mothership of Christianity, and the Protestant and Evangelical churches are an awesome fleet following the Mothership (or maybe trying to lead!). They are all headed in the right direction because they are Christian.

One of the main things to understand is the tremendous good the churches and the clergy have done over the years. Most priests, pastors, and ministers are selflessly devoted to their flock. They deal on a personal level with people in all the most important moments of their lives. We tend to hear more about the bad apples and forget about all the good.

A great way to start on this path is to find a friend of yours who is a committed Christian. The evangelicals are particularly good at this. Ask them about the impact of faith on their life and outlook for the future. *Be curious about spirituality!* It is an important subject. Many different things can inspire curiosity. Most of all, curiosity about Jesus Christ.

This will lead to a spiritual openness and possibility of personal and spiritual change.

Ultimately, your baby steps will lead to a personal relationship with Jesus like so many others before you. It is much more than just acceptance and knowledge of faith. It is a way of life providing purpose, personal development, service to others, joy, and peace.

CHURCH: DO I HAVE TO GO?

I am going to repeat this quote from Chapter 10 because of its significance.

> *Christianity, if false, is of no importance, and if true, of infinite importance. The only thing it cannot be is moderately important.*
>
> **C.S. LEWIS**

Yet I'm afraid many people act as if it is moderately important.

Do I even have to join a church? Can't I just live my life as a Christian? This is a question that I used to always ask my mother. Why should I have to go to that church with all those strangers? Can't I just find God in nature or on the golf course? It's a pretty good question. But the answer is no, not really. Jesus set up a Church in the first place because He knows that we have this tendency toward rebellion and sin going back thousands of years.

Going to church at least once a week keeps us on track instead of veering off or petering out. It's a great way to thank God for another week that we have survived this world and for the many good things that have happened to us. We don't necessarily go to church to get something out of it, although we often do. We go there to thank God and fulfill the Third Commandment *Thou Keep Holy the Lord's Day.* The fact that God made it one of the Ten Commandments is the ultimate reason we go to church. It is obedience to our Creator.

AFTERWORD

The conclusion? Yes, there is a God! Not only is there a God … but as shown here there *must* be a God.

But there is a crisis of faith in the Western world. Tragic spiritual and moral decline. Attack on Christian values and morality, marriage, and sex. We are losing our sense of sin, and we think if we ignore the reality of sin, it will go away. God detests the denial of sin even more than sin because we remove God from the picture.

The culture has evangelized the people of God more than the people of God have evangelized the culture. Whether we know it or not we are participants in a great spiritual battle where the playing field is Earth.

Are you one of the people of God? Do you call upon the name of the Lord, or do you call upon the name of men? Or yourself?

What hope do we have besides the promise of Jesus Christ through his life, death, and resurrection? The answer is none. But with Jesus, we can do all. There are those who think the answer is artificial intelligence and depopulation. This is pitiful.

Why dost thou persecute me?

Acts 9:4

The problem is one of faith. We would be more inclined to live according to God's laws if we really believed in Him. Faith, as we have shown in these pages, can begin with reason and logic. I pray that this will be the stepping-stone for many who read this toward belief in God and His Son, Jesus Christ.

> *When the Son of Man comes,*
> *will he find faith on earth?*
>
> **LUKE 18:8**

Atheists reason that, somehow, they know. Agnostics reason that they don't know. This makes sense at first, but then they default to the atheist's worldview.

Why does God want us to believe even more than to avoid sin?

It is because if we don't believe, we remove ourselves from God's judgment. We live by our own code, not God's code.

The fact that God stresses the point means that He gives us all the means to believe. He has done everything he can to save us given that we have free will.

There have been thousands — perhaps millions — of instantaneous conversions to Christ over the past 2,000 years, beginning with Saint Paul, who was literally knocked off his horse and blinded by the resurrected Jesus. Jesus told him Saul: you are playing for the wrong team. Why are you persecuting me?

THIS IS AN INVITATION TO BE ON GOD'S TEAM

All you really need to do is open your mind and soften your heart; you're pretty much there.

He empowers us—leading and encouraging but allowing the battles and leading us in our weakness into trust.

My grace is sufficient.

2 Corinthians 12:9

ABOUT THE AUTHOR

The Logic That God Exists, is the first book Bob Trussell has written, but it is one that he has been mulling in his head for many years. While engaging in the business world and helping to raise a family, Trussell observed the culture often leaving God out of the equation. He felt called to do something about it. It seemed to him that the fundamental issue was people had lost some faith in the existence of God.

Trussell was heavily involved in the thoroughbred racehorse business from college to about 40 years old when he went through a crisis. The horse business went through a severe recession, and the only means of supporting his young family evaporated. Seeking answers, he fell back on his Catholic upbringing, he turned to prayer, and asked for a way out of the predicament. Within a couple of years of saying yes to new opportunities and trying various entrepreneurial ventures unsuccessfully, he believes a miracle happened—a totally unexpected answer to his prayers.

Through his French horse trainer Alain Falourd and his Swedish horse chiropractor friend, Trussell met a Swedish man in the racing world named Mikael Magnusson, a successful entrepreneur and horseman who also claimed to make the world's greatest mattress. Indeed, he did, and Trussell obtained North American distribution rights for this product, which became known as Tempur-Pedic. Ten years later, he rang the New York Stock Exchange bell when Tempur-Pedic went public for a $1.4 billion valuation. Full of gratitude, Trussell hopes that at least one person will come to find God as a result of this book.

You can hear the whole story on NPR's *How I Built This* podcast with Guy Raz.

Trussell has three children and lives in Lexington, Kentucky, with his wife Martha. They are enjoying their first grandchild, Grace.

You can contact Bob or ask further questions at:

THELOGICTHATGODEXISTS.COM

THELOGICTHATGODEXISTS@PROTON.ME

Sophia Institute

SOPHIA INSTITUTE IS A nonprofit institution that seeks to nurture the spiritual, moral, and cultural life of souls and to spread the gospel of Christ in conformity with the authentic teachings of the Roman Catholic Church.

Sophia Institute Press fulfills this mission by offering translations, reprints, and new publications that afford readers a rich source of the enduring wisdom of mankind.

Sophia Institute also operates the popular online resource CatholicExchange.com. *Catholic Exchange* provides world news from a Catholic perspective as well as daily devotionals and articles that will help readers to grow in holiness and live a life consistent with the teachings of the Church.

In 2013, Sophia Institute launched Sophia Institute for Teachers to renew and rebuild Catholic culture through service to Catholic education. With the goal of nurturing the spiritual, moral, and cultural life of souls, and an abiding respect for the role and work of teachers, we strive to provide materials and programs that are at once enlightening to the mind and ennobling to the heart; faithful and complete, as well as useful and practical.

Sophia Institute gratefully recognizes the Solidarity Association for preserving and encouraging the growth of our apostolate over the course of many years. Without their generous and timely support, this book would not be in your hands.

www.SophiaInstitute.com
www.CatholicExchange.com
www.SophiaInstituteforTeachers.org

Sophia Institute Press is a registered trademark of Sophia Institute.
Sophia Institute is a tax-exempt institution as defined by the
Internal Revenue Code, Section 501(c)(3). Tax ID 22-2548708.